The Art of
Mandala Meditation

Mandala Designs to Heal Your Mind, Body, and Spirit

MICHAL BEAUCAIRE   Artwork by Paul Heussenstamm

Published by
Adams Media, a division of F+W Media, Inc.
57 Littlefield Street, Avon, MA 02322. U.S.A.
www.adamsmedia.com

ISBN 10: 1-4405-4114-0
ISBN 13: 978-1-4405-4114-8
eISBN 10: 1-4405-4388-7
eISBN 13: 978-1-4405-4388-3

Printed in China.

10 9 8 7 6 5 4 3 2 1

This book is intended as general information only, and should not be used to diagnose or treat any health condition. In light of the complex, individual, and specific nature of health problems, this book is not intended to replace professional medical advice. The ideas, procedures, and suggestions in this book are intended to supplement, not replace, the advice of a trained medical professional. Consult your physician before adopting any of the suggestions in this book, as well as about any condition that may require diagnosis or medical attention. The author and publisher disclaim any liability arising directly or indirectly from the use of this book.

This publication is designed to provide accurate and authoritative information with regard to the subject matter covered. It is sold with the understanding that the publisher is not engaged in rendering legal, accounting, or other professional advice. If legal advice or other expert assistance is required, the services of a competent professional person should be sought.

—From a *Declaration of Principles* jointly adopted by a Committee of the American Bar Association and a Committee of Publishers and Associations

Many of the designations used by manufacturers and sellers to distinguish their product are claimed as trademarks. Where those designations appear in this book and Adams Media was aware of a trademark claim, the designations have been printed with initial capital letters.

Previously published in Hebrew in 2008.

Originally published by Orion Publishing House, *www.orion-books.co.il*

Artwork by Paul Heussenstamm, Laguna Beach, CA: *www.Mandalas.com*

Graphic design: Hafuch Studio, Shirit Cohen: hafuch@netvision.net.il

Translation: Dr. Orly Doron, PhD; Pamela A. Lord: *orgold@gmail.com*

For free consulting with the author, Michal Beaucaire, please e-mail *argaman@netvision.net.il*.

This book is available at quantity discounts for bulk purchases.
For information, please call 1-800-289-0963.

Special thanks

Special thanks to my husband Abraham and to my children for the privilege of having you as part of my life.

When my son Yehuda was five years old, we went for a vacation and stayed in a hotel on the beach. Our room was located on the first floor. As we went to the balcony, we could see many cars driving on the main road. The balcony was full of sand that had blown over from the seashore, and Yehuda climbed on the chair to look outside. His few steps left footprints in the sand on the balcony floor.

"Mom!" He happily told me his discovery, "When I was watching the world, I left footprints!"

I wish for all of you, that when you watch the world, you will leave footprints. Do things in order to change and to improve our world!

Michal

Paul Heussenstamm

I have put into words what I've been exploring over the course of some fifty years of life. During that time, much of it spent becoming and being an artist, I have come to know the soul, and I have come to understand that the journey of THE ARTIST is the discovery of the soul.

For me, finding, facing, and knowing your soul is the ultimate purpose in life. This is the foundation of all my teaching, be it through painting, writing, or simply living life. Learning to see with your heart's soul, as an artist, is the result of a long transformation, an evolution from a business life to a creative life. After years of developing and practicing the medium of painting, I am able to share the path to the heart through the soul. I am able to communicate the range of feeling and seeing that I experience day by day, both in my artwork and in my life.

For instance, the soul is outside of time and space. Sharing a communication directly from the soul creates a dynamism based on the difficult task of attempting to explain what appears to be invisible. Yet sharing from the soul's eyes reveals a depth and perception not available to ordinary eyesight. So only with the long body of this journal, along with my own long journey, can we truly understand the realm of the soul and its value to all artists.

In my experience, the soul is the artist and true art merely passes through the artist. Our infrastructure of museums and the societal-based valuation of art are, in fact, soul-based. It follows that the heart can be used continually as a soul organ for perceiving the value and sacred nature of soul art.

I use the teachings of famous and honored artists throughout time to amplify and explain how the soul cooperates in the paintings, teachings, and lives of these masters.

During the twenty-five years of my business career, I felt that something major that lived at a certain depth was missing from my life. Though I always felt creative, I now realize that I was not consciously connected to my living soul. This connection developed over time as a result of artistic exploration, numerous epiphanies, countless inspirations, the blessed intervention of teachers, synchronistic events, unexpected pain and loss, and most importantly through endless hours of painting and exploration in my own studio.

It has become my deep desire to share my life's work, to express what I see and feel in the mystery of painting, and to help others make similar connections. I truly feel that once you have been given the gift of seeing the mystery, of a direct connection to the Divine, this experience will be sufficient to fuel an entire lifetime of creatively revealing and translating, through art, your own spiritually based experiences.

It has been my destiny to achieve a radical personal transformation from a business life to a creative life and, finally, to a spiritual life through ART. When I first began to paint, I didn't see the soul or realize my soul's desire for my life. I didn't know that I had already begun my search. It was through painting that my inner eyes began to open and, miraculously, began to see the SOUL!

I have learned that once we have seen the soul in multiple ways and on different levels, it has a profound and direct influence on our lives. I have found the presence of the soul to be prevalent in paintings and in the lives of artists through the centuries. Painting is the journey of the artist searching to reveal that which he both feels and sees. Picasso found that, "Painting is a blind man's profession. He paints not what he sees, but what he feels." In my own experience I have learned that art is the soul manifesting in time and space.

When we learn how to open to the soul, we begin to feel connected with it, like a Buddhist practicing nonduality. First, we connect in our paintings, and then we connect to life.

I share many of my findings and discoveries of other great artists as a way to further strengthen my teaching that art reveals the soul. I understand that some of what I am saying will seem very different from our society's common thinking, but I am sharing the soul's wisdom. Simply put, the soul's wisdom is the essence of my life. Here, my work will be to put into words a way of seeing and connecting to life. My teaching is to reveal a new reality (soul) at all levels, in this writing as in my painting and in my life, just as it exists in TRUE works of art.

Michelangelo found that, "good painting is nothing but a copy of the perfection of God." In my experience, from a soul level, the Divine is working mysteriously through the soul in all true works of art.

The soul naturally connects, unifies, and sees in patterns. We have to know this to enter her realms!

Paul Heussenstamm

Contents

Meditations for Fun

Getting Started

What Is Meditation?

Meditation causes the brain to operate on an alpha wavelength. Alpha waves are slow-frequency waves with a high rate of electricity that appear when the body is in a state of relaxation. They constitute one of the stages of slumber. Their frequency at first is of 8–13 Hz, which gradually decreases to a frequency of 8–10 Hz as the body enters a state of deeper sleep, causing the heartbeat to drop and the muscles to relax. Although dream-like illusions occur, this is not real sleep.

The objective of meditation is to raise the brain to an alpha wave frequency while in a wakeful state. Being in such a state for lengthy periods every day makes a person calm and relaxed.

How can you reach an alpha wave frequency without actually falling asleep? Try closing your eyes and recalling a recent vacation in a location that you love to visit. Focus your thoughts on the time you spent there until you can actually sense the feeling of wind in your hair and the smell of the ocean. That moment is when you have reached a state of meditation; in other words, you have transferred your brain to an alpha wave frequency.

Guided Imagery

There are various kinds of meditation, all of which move the brain to an alpha wave frequency. My own favorite form of meditation consists of guided imagery, which leads you to a state of relaxation and moves the brain to an alpha wave frequency via clearly defined, sentence-by-sentence instructions.

With this method, you are able, undisturbed, to imagine and focus on a specific situation. There are brief interludes between one directive and another, in which you can experience the last directive issued. The guided imagery method is most appropriate for periods of heightened stress that allow you little time to devote to yourself, or to relax and to focus on pleasant thoughts.

Guided imagery is usually used when you want to go on a spiritual journey to a magical garden, to a quiet corner with beautiful flowers, where you hear the lovely notes of a harp and birds chirping in the background, and see a magic chest that contains an important message. In this book, I have adapted this system and turned it into a healing method for self-reinforcement.

I hope you connect with this idea and enjoy every minute of the experience.

How Does Meditation Help?

The alpha wave frequency, which is where the brain is during meditation, allows us to imprint new behavioral concepts that we have not experienced in the past. We all know about the characteristics inherent in us—behavior, reactions, harmful behavioral traits—but we don't always know how to conquer or change them.

For example, hasn't everyone tried—at least once in his or her life—to follow a diet, to stop smoking, or not to get angry for a whole day? At certain times in our lives, we have all tried to shake off undesirable habits, only to discover how hard this is; indeed, almost impossible.

Meditation can help. The positive thinking that is part of the meditation practice and the emotional calm that envelops you as you practice meditation give you the ability to cope with the undesirable aspects of life, including illness.

An Original Concept

Meditation is not meant only for people who have visited the Far East and wear loose clothes and hang colorful chains around their necks; nor does it necessary require you to float above the floor in a lotus position in order to reap its benefits. Meditation is a tool for achieving objectives and fulfilling dreams; it can be used by anyone who seeks spiritual elevation and change.

For me, meditation is a way of life and I practice it not only when I am sitting alone, quietly, for a few moments. The power of thought also serves me in seemingly trivial day-to-day activity. For example, let's say I anticipate a problem finding a parking space near a place I have to get to. Even before I start the car, I close my eyes and imagine the free parking space waiting patiently for my arrival. You are welcome to try it. If I think of someone who isn't feeling well and imagine him or her getting better, standing up on his or her feet and functioning as normal, the energy generated by these thoughts helps them toward a swift recovery. This works on every level in my life.

Meditation requires no previous experience, only a desire to try it. Desire is the key to success.
This book will teach you a new and positive approach to life. In time you will internalize it and it will fill your life with a sense of joy and self-fulfillment. The objective is to create a positive thought process, because it is thought that creates and forms reality. Persevere and you will see that it is so.

The meditations in this book are to be practiced with your eyes open, gazing straight at the center of the mandala, but not focusing on it. Focusing on your breathing and following the written instructions is very relaxing and will serve you in every moment of your life.

What Is a Mandala?

Mandala is a Sanskrit word: *manda* = essence, *la* = within; it is a circle that contains the essence.

A mandala is a shape or an element in nature, taking the form of a circle, symmetrically from outside in, and providing a sense of movement and harmony between the elements. Nature has many varied mandala-like structures; for example, the trunk cross-section of a fallen tree, with its ever-increasing circles fanning out from the center; the exquisite formation of the lotus flower; and many more.

The mandala symbolizes the laws of the universe and, since man is a microcosm of the universe, many cultures believe that the mandala also symbolizes the human soul. The mandala comes to us from India and Tibet; however, it has also been found in other cultures of the world, e.g., Native Americans, Australian Aboriginals, and others.

Why Should I Look at the Mandala?

The brain consists of three centers that are responsible for three dimensions: concentration, focus, and parameter. In order to function successfully and competently, an efficient internal communication must exist among these three dimensions.

Let's deal here with the dimension of concentration, which is relevant to us and which is responsible for order and organization—the ability to organize thoughts, to file things away, and to generally put our lives in order. Also, there is a physiological connection to the balance between the upper and lower parts of the body and long-term memory, which makes it possible to combine work on feelings and logic. When we are feeling stressed, the concentration dimension loses its balance. On the other hand, when we are focused and organized, our feelings and logic are in harmony and there is a sense of balance; we have both feet on the ground. By watching the mandala, the brain shifts more easily into an alpha wave frequency, to a state of inner calm and relaxation and to experience meditation as it is being created, as it is being colored, or as it is being observed. The sense of inner peace is a result of the mandala's properties, neutralizing the causes of stress and helping to reorder our thoughts.

Some experts recommend that people and children who suffer from ADHD should draw and color mandalas as a type of art therapy. Looking at a mandala before going into a lesson can help these children to be more composed in class.

Why Draw a Mandala?

Physiologically, by drawing a mandala you are activating your brain's right hemisphere (which is responsible for emotions, feelings, imagination, and associations), thereby making it possible for the left hemisphere (which rules your linear reasoning and problem solving) to rest.

When drawing a personal mandala, we connect with our inner truth by figuratively weeding the path clear to our hidden treasures, those gifts that we were given when we were born. We reveal our artistic side, unblock our energy paths, and heal ourselves. The connection to colors and to various lines and shapes allows us to join those frequencies that we need to experience balance. According to the holistic approach, balance means healing.

How to Use This Book

Usually, people turn to books only when they encounter problems, but in truth when we are really in need, we have neither the patience nor the mindset to start leafing through a book in search of the meditation most appropriate for any given situation. I suggest preparing yourself in advance. Carefully read through the table of contents of this book and check off or make a separate list of those things that you would like to change and improve in yourself over the following few weeks. For example: If you have a tendency to sink into depression, make a check next to Joy and Happiness, which is a mood-enhancing meditation. If you are having difficulties sticking to a diet, practice a daily Weight Loss meditation. You could also choose an additional meditation, such as Beauty or Attracting Your Soul Mate.

- Using these meditations on a daily basis will ensure you a unique experience and positive results.
- Leave the book in a prominent place and meditation will become a part of your daily routine. Forgetfulness is our greatest enemy.
- I recommend that you change your meditations monthly and choose new issues on which to work. The greater your spiritual development, the more you will feel the need to work on your inner self— on deeper levels and on different personality traits. **This need indicates that inner change is taking place. It's wonderful!**

What Does Each Meditation Contain?

1. Most of the meditations emphasize the awareness necessary for each particular meditation. For example, if you choose a meditation for Deep Sleep, you will be able to understand which positive awareness you should connect to before going to sleep.
2. Meditations for the Body contains explanations drawn from various schools of thought worldwide that believe illness does not erupt without an emotional or spiritual reason, and that the quickest and most effective cures come from discovering and dealing with the reason for the illness. Also, this section explains how each illness is given to us in order to bring about a spiritual awakening, so that we may begin to ask the right questions regarding our lives and choices and our ability to repair them. An open-minded approach to the advice offered might reveal to you the source of your problem and its remedy.
3. Following every meditation, there is a mandala. As you meditate, you should look into the center of the mandala and breathe deeply, following the directions in the text. This is the color therapy state, taken from energetic healing, and it is an inseparable part of the meditation. I also advise that you wear clothing of the same colors shown in the mandala that relates to the meditation of your choice.
4. All the meditations in this book are relaxing. By watching the mandala that accompanies the meditation, your brain is readily transferred to an alpha wave frequency.
5. As you read the meditation, close your eyes after every step, imagine each and every aspect of it, then open your eyes and continue to the next step.
6. If you feel connected to a specific mandala, but its instructions are not relevant to your needs, you may watch it for as long as you like, even if you are not meditating on it with the text.

How Long Should a Meditation Last?

The minimum time necessary to practice a particular meditation is stated in the instructions for each one. If you have the time, take longer—take as long as you wish; do not restrict yourself.

Keeping Comfortable While Meditating

The position of your body is very important when meditating. Any kind of discomfort is liable to disturb the efficiency of the meditation. It is best to be seated in a comfortable armchair; this enables you to look at the book and, when necessary, to close your eyes. You can lean your head back and enjoy every minute.

Your body is a circle of energy, you could say, of electricity; if you fold your arms, or cross your fingers, or cross your legs, you are preventing the circular flow of energy through your body. My advice, therefore, is to relax your legs, to lay your feet on the floor, and to place your hands, palms up, near your hips. You can, if you like, lay this book on your open hands.

How Can I Stop My Thoughts While Meditating?

When you are preparing to meditate, you may find that all kinds of thoughts crowd their way into your mind. I wonder why . . .

Well, I have an easy and convenient way to dampen these thoughts; you are welcome to try it. Close your eyes and without straining them, squint into the bridge of your nose, to the highest point you can reach between your eyebrows. At this point, there are no thoughts.

As soon as you feel calmer, release the squint and sink deep into a sweet meditation.

Healing Stones and Crystals

Each crystal and healing stone possesses an energy frequency. The combination of light and the reflected energy of a crystal creates a healing frequency that is especially beneficial. When you lay a crystal on your body, it opens this special energy and lets it flow into you, particularly if the same frequency in your body is weak for some reason. This new flow of energy hastens the process of healing and balances your body and soul.

It is possible and even advisable to use several different crystals simultaneously. On the other hand, you don't have to use crystals at all; it is merely a suggestion.

Each of the meditations in this book suggests specific healing stones that are most appropriate for the body parts that are being treated. You can lay the stones at the appropriate energy centers (chakras), or simply hold them in your hand. You may also drink an infusion of healing stones, according to the following instructions.

Preparing an Infusion of Healing Stones and Crystals

Place the stones in a glass full of drinking water and place a saucer on top. Leave to infuse for at least four hours and then drink the water. After using the crystal, rinse it in tap water and dry it on a windowsill. You should drink at least one such infusion every day, in order to gauge its effect.

More information on healing stones and crystals can be found in *Love Is in the Earth*, by Melody (Earth Love Publishing House).

The Energy Centers—Chakras

The human body has seven energy centers known as chakras. *Chakra* is a Sanskrit word meaning wheel, or "disc," or "turning." The Indians discovered that the energy in these centers is circular, moving from each center outward, creating an aura (the electromagnetic field surrounding us). Each of the energy centers is filled with a different color, according to the colors of the rainbow: purple, blue, light blue, green, yellow, orange, and red. When all our chakras are open and active, and energy flows through them, a white aura surrounds our bodies. Unfortunately, a study of the hundreds of people who attended my lectures and workshops shows that the average number of chakras open at one time is only between two and three.

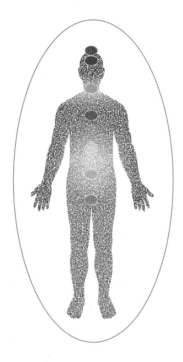

What Does This Mean?

When a chakra is closed, its color will not be reflected in our aura, which means that our aura lacks energy, and will not provide us with a perfect protective covering. After about five years of insufficient energy in one of our chakras, our body usually begins to broadcast signals, in the form of vague aches and pains. If you are in tune with your body, these signals are a warning bell and, if they are ignored, they only grow stronger.

Your objective is to maintain a perfect energy level in your body, to keep energy flowing through the chakras; only then can you maintain your health and well-being.

The Crown Chakra

Purple in color, it is located at the top of the head. The sound that opens this chakra is OM. This chakra influences the head, thought, and memory; the two spheres of the brain; and the ability to analyze new ideas and to turn them into practice. Via this energy center, you can connect to a higher dimension through meditation; cure headaches, migraines, and epilepsy; and achieve a deeper sleep. It also helps with dyslexia, and ADHD, and soothes hyperactivity.

The Brow Chakra

Blue in color, it is located in the center of the forehead, between the eyebrows. The note that opens this chakra is OM. This chakra affects the eyes, ears, sinuses, and nose, and it helps promote sleep. Through this "third eye," it is possible to connect to an enhanced intuition and to develop messages and communication.

The Throat Chakra

A clear sky blue in color, this chakra is located at the base of the throat. The note that opens this chakra is HAM. It affects the throat, gums, tonsils, esophagus, back of the neck, shoulders, the thyroid gland, and the ability to communicate and express oneself. It enhances your ability to talk about things that trouble you. The flow of energy in this chakra can be opened through discourse and discussion of issues you find difficult to cope with.

The Heart Chakra

Typically colored green, pink, and turquoise, the heart chakra is located in the center of the chest. The note that opens it is YAM. Of all the colors, green is the one used in balancing and healing; in healing it is used for transferring therapeutic energy. It is in the center of the color spectrum. Note: Green is not suitable for use on cancer patients, because it is responsible for growth and regeneration.

Pink is the color responsible for the emotional aspect surrounding the heart and **turquoise** is especially influential on your sense of freedom, as well as on your lungs and breathing. The heart chakra affects the heart, lungs, breasts, thymus gland, immune system, arms, hands, and, from an emotional point of view, it includes and maintains all our feelings, disappointments, and the emotional burden we carry with us throughout our lives.

We can compare our heart to an onion that has a large, well-polished diamond at its center that cannot be seen because of the many protective layers that cover it. These layers are similar to those that we all form around our hearts, each layer symbolizing a moving or painful event. In time, these layers turn into a block of insensitivity and a general feeling of ennui that contrasts with our past. In order to live life to the fullest, to enjoy every minute, to love and be loved; in order to notice a new flower in the garden and to enjoy the sunrise, you must decide to peel away those defensive layers, and to move forward toward emotional maturity. As you proceed with this process, you'll experience a new and better life that will enable you to cope with every problem you encounter. You should seek a connection to your heart and strive to connect to the diamond that lies in the heart of each of us, and not to the layers of onion that form a gloomy shroud.

The Solar Plexus Chakra

Yellow in color, the solar plexus is located in the upper abdomen. The note that opens it is RAM. The solar plexus contains our ego, our desires, and our ambition. All the potential you own is expressed in this center. If you wish to strengthen your self-confidence and to succeed in your endeavors, you have to reinforce the energy in this chakra, which affects all your internal organs and more: liver, spleen, gall bladder, pancreas, stomach, duodenum, small intestine, kidneys, and urinary tract. According to alternative medicine, all our rage is concentrated in the liver, so if you tend to feel angry, avoid wearing yellow clothes. Instead, you should choose shades of lime green.

The essence of "I" is connected to this chakra. But beware! Although it is our ego that urges us and pushes us toward success, it can also place obstacles in our way, if it gets out of proportion and forces us beyond our limits. Among the obstacles placed by the ego are such statements as: "I am the most important person in the world," "Who is he/she to tell me what to do?" (especially if it's your boss), and other sentences that come from a place that is not particularly positive. Negative feelings also create obstacles.

The Sacral Chakra

This chakra is orange colored and is located two fingers beneath the navel. The note that opens this chakra is VAM. It affects the female organs and more: uterus, ovaries, fallopian tubes, large intestines, and pelvis. It fills with energy when we are happy. Orange is the color of happiness and I recommend you wear it whenever possible. It has the ability to take you out of a depressed state and improve your mood. The energy in this center is reduced when you are unhappy or when you feel stuck with no enthusiasm for anything. Most of the people I examined had a blocked sacral chakra; which is why so many suffer from lower-back pain; a lack of energy in any of the centers eventually causes physical pain.

The Base Chakra

Colored red, the base chakra is located on the coccyx, the last bone in the spinal column. The note that opens this chakra is LAM.

Red is the color that encourages warmth and is therefore unsuitable for people who are hot-tempered or quickly angered; nor is it good for people who are hyperactive, since it would raise their activity level and make them more restless. Nor is the color red suitable for cancer patients, since it encourages spreading. Instead of red, use orange or brown.

In men, the base chakra affects the prostate gland and the male reproductive organs, the lower spine, legs, knees and feet, fears and anxieties, violent tendencies, instinctive reactions, and restlessness. It also helps those of us who have our heads in the clouds to get our feet back on terra firma.

How Can I Use the Chakras to Open My Energy Flow?

The first option is to wear the colors representing chakras you need to open. Preferably, each color should be worn near the relevant chakra; for example: a green shirt and red pants (if they clash, you could wear each garment alternately). Another option is to place an appropriate healing stone on the chakra through which you want energy to flow; for this you should lie down, breathing deeply, for ten to twenty minutes a day. A third option is to imagine that you are surrounded by the color of the chakra and inhaling the color deep into your body, then exhaling the air from the chakra (you can use the drawing of the chakras in this chapter). After a meditation like this, the chakra remains balanced and flowing.

Joy, Laughter, and Music

These three things have a positive and therapeutic effect on your body and soul. Research shows that after a healthy laugh, the blood contains an increased amount of antibodies and cells that protect it against viruses, germs, and cancer cells; endorphins are released by the brain, which actually alleviate pain and induce a wonderful feeling of well-being; the stomach muscles and the diaphragm gently massage the abdominal organs and help digestion. In addition, you are more relaxed, more satisfied, and more patient; you sleep better; and you are more creative after a good laugh. Like laughter, joy and music seep deep into every cell in your body, infusing it with equilibrium where there is imbalance, reinforcing weak spots, and serving your body and mind as wonderful assistants.

I strongly recommend joining a laughter yoga workshop, where you will learn how to laugh even when there is no real reason to do so. It is a good idea, too, to watch funny movies with a happy ending, to go to standup comedy shows, to subscribe to the comedy TV channels, and to listen to a lot of music. Some kinds of music are especially helpful in healing the body and repairing the structure of damaged cells; these include classical music, Irish/Celtic music, Japanese Hado music, and any other kind of heavenly music that plucks at the strings of the soul.

Healthy Movement

Gentle and relaxing physical activity—such as yoga, Feldenkrais technique, tai-chi, and chi kong (qigong)—opens the flow of energy and allows the body to wind down and the soul to open up. That is good for everyone!

Get to Know Your Body and Your Organs

Meditation is aimed at healing certain parts of your body by focusing your thoughts on them. It is therefore necessary to become familiar with the organ you want to heal. You might even keep a drawing of it in this book or in your pocket, so it will be constantly at hand. The more familiar you are with the organ, the quicker and better the results of your meditation will be.

Ritual Immersion: Spiritual and Energetic Purification

If you are seeking spiritual purification, a ritual immersion is a good option for you. The person who emerges from such a dip is not the same as the one who entered it. Holding your breath as you enter the water is tantamount to stopping your life; re-emerging from the water is the same as returning to life. It is recommended, therefore, that each time you take a ritual immersion, you decide to start to live anew. You can dip effectively in the sea, a lake, a spring, or anywhere else into which rainwater or dew flows merged. (An indoor heated pool will not do for this ritual.) You can use an outdoor pool, but a natural source of water is always best because it is there that the energies for healing and rebirth you are looking for can be found. The search for such a source will in itself

infuse you with extra energy. A low water temperature will increase the energy that you'll receive, since the harder it is for you to enter the water, the greater your struggle against your natural desire to seek comfort. By struggling against your nature, you are increasing your efforts to find change or healing, which in turn increases the amount and quality of the energy you achieve. Why settle for less?

Wear a swimsuit or loose clothing, remove all jewelry, and let your hair hang loose. You should immerse yourself completely in the water, which must cover every part of your body. When the water is especially cold (in the winter) you should go in as far as your pelvis and then simply sit in the water.

How Many Times Should I Immerse Myself?

For your first time, one immersion is enough. It becomes easier in subsequent baths and you can gradually increase the number of full immersions. Here are some options for energetic immersion: three times to achieve equilibrium; seven times for healing; ten times for perfection.

What Should I Think about as I Immerse Myself?

Be aware that the water in which you are immersing your body completely changes your energy. You must imagine that all your accumulated negative energy (e.g., your anger, illnesses, or discomfort that is burdening your heart, or anything else that you want to dispose of) is flowing out of you and into the water the moment you immerse yourself. You should imagine everything dark in your energy becoming light, and in your subsequent immersions, you should imagine yourself filling with light, a light that is being absorbed into every cell in your body.

Pregnant women should immerse daily. Immersion will maintain your peace of mind, which means that your unborn baby will be calm and relaxed and will remain so after birth.

I immerse myself all year round, whenever I get the chance. This, and the effort entailed in immersing myself in cold water even in the winter when the hills opposite my home are covered in snow, has enabled me to recover and to rid myself completely of a large 1.2-inch growth in my armpit, and to become pregnant at the ages of forty and forty-two, despite my doctors' doubts. I had only one ovary and irregular menstruation (you can read the whole story in my book *Therefore Choose Life: Healing and Recuperation from Cancer with Guided Imagery*, which describes my complete recovery).

Healing by Drinking Water

According to the German physician Dr. Hammond of IBN-Sina Healthcare International, a daily intake of six glasses of water brings almost complete recovery from almost any illness. The idea is to drink water as soon as you rise in the morning, even before brushing your teeth, and to refrain from coffee or food for an hour after drinking water.

Dr. Hammond reports that water therapy can cure the following illnesses: constipation, acid reflux, hypertension, diabetes, general tension, sinusitis, bronchitis, fatigue, tuberculosis, meningitis, kidney stones, urinary tract infections, obesity, rheumatism, arthritis, muscular pain, cancer (breast, cervical, leukemia, stomach, and intestinal), throat infections, headaches, redness in the eyes, coughs, irregular menses, gastric infections, anemia, and asthma.

How to Drink

Hammond's recommended dose is four successive glasses of water with a ten-minute break, followed by two more glasses. It is not easy to get used to drinking large quantities of water. You might feel sick or have a strong desire for your usual cup of coffee. I can personally testify that after two days of this regimen, I was able to reject coffee and I experienced a change in my awareness of food. My body demanded only food that is healthy; I ate less and was driven to energetic exercise. Another side effect of drinking water is a heightened alertness that replaced the previous sluggishness I experienced after every meal. People who are not used to drinking water at all (like I was) will find that this water regimen will actually increase your need for water.

Recovery

The results of this regimen are quick to show. According to Dr. Hammond, after one day, constipation is alleviated (although, of course, treatment must continue). After two days, acid reflux will disappear. After a week, you can cure diabetes. Cancer is cured after one month, and hypertension and pneumonia are cured after three months of a strict water regimen. People suffering from cancer and arthritis should follow the regimen three times a day, morning, noon, and night. My experience shows that it is enough to restrict the water regimen to mornings only if necessary, however; this is just as effective with the groups of recovering cancer patients I teach and there is no extra pressure on the kidneys.

If you think about it, the system is really very logical and very simple. Just three weeks after beginning the regimen, I felt several very positive changes in my health; for example: the pains I had in my neck had disappeared, the tendonitis in my upper arm disappeared and no longer hurt, I am much more alert than before, my facial skin has greatly improved, my bowel movements are regular, and I have reduced my coffee intake to one cup a day.

How Can I Tell If This Regimen Isn't Good for Me?

This water regime is not suitable for those suffering from kidney problems, heart conditions, edema, or high blood pressure. If you experience swelling anywhere on your body immediately after drinking large quantities of water, or if your urine disposal does not follow the same pace as your water intake, give your doctor a call.

What Kind of Water Is Best?

Any water you prefer. If you are fortunate enough to have good tap water, you may drink that.

When Should I Stop?

I see no reason to stop at all. Why stop something that is so beneficial for you? I wrote about this water therapy in my self-awareness column in the local paper. The article inspired many, and the whole town was on water therapy by the end of the week. I received dozens of calls from people who had read the article and passed it on to others, so that it ended up being read by several thousand people. Everyone asked me to give them a discount in the number of glasses of water they should drink and in the length of time they had to wait for their cup of coffee or food. But if you, too, are hoping for a reduction—well, you can reduce

the number of cups to four, but you can't drink it *after* your cup of coffee—sorry. I hope you, too, will benefit from the full regimen.

Messages from Water

Water equals sharing, flowing; it is the truly physical thing in our world that is closest in its composition to the eternal light, to the energy that spreads and diffuses and gives of itself to everyone. The effect water has on the body is enormous.

In his book, *Messages from Water*, Dr. Masaru Emoto sums up his research of the molecular composition of water in various situations. For example: water at its source, in comparison with the same water when it reaches a lake after it runs through the city; or water whose molecular composition changes when it is addressed in words such as "thank you," "love," "angel," as opposed to negative words, such as "you are disgusting," "idiot," or "I hate you." The positive words create diamond-shaped molecules, whereas the negative words caused the water molecules to be murky and disordered. His book provides a picture of two jars of cooked rice; one of them was addressed each morning as "idiot," while the other was told "thank you very much." The rice in the first jar turned black and rotted, while in the second jar, the rice took on a pleasant, very special scent and it stayed fresh for a week. Dr. Emoto's book contains many pictures that illustrate water molecules under different circumstances.

How Can I Use Water Messaging in My Daily Life?

1. Stick labels on the bottles you are drinking your water from, writing on them positive words such

as "love," "thank you," "health," etc. Be sure the words are facing inward toward the bottle and the water.

2. Think positively when you are cooking and talk lovingly to your food. Think of harmony in your family.

3. Connect these conclusions to the fact that the human body consists of 73 percent water and that might encourage you to change the way you speak. Use positive words more often, and you can change the molecular structure of the water in your body, and heal yourself and those in your vicinity.

Sharing

The greatest charge of energy comes from sharing. That is an idea that takes a while to absorb, but I believe that once you have studied the idea of sharing (by reading this book), you will internalize it and put it to good use.

Real sharing, with no alternative motives or agenda, is quite difficult and does not come naturally to most people. In my workshops, there is always someone who resists my teachings. Yet people tend to believe that they are constantly in a state of sharing, helping everyone, always willing to lend a helping hand under all circumstances.

The truth is that only people born under the sign of Pisces can be in full sharing-mode, but this is a trait they were born with, which makes it easy for them. They even share too much, to the extent that they are often exploited. People born under other zodiac signs seem to be more involved in themselves and are unable to care for others. According to most of the sharers, they always help when they are asked to,

but the ideal of real sharing is to ask someone if he needs help, to care for someone even before being asked to.

If we change our attitude and start thinking of others more than of ourselves, we shall be protected and our immune system will not be obliged to deal with illness—we'll be strong and healthy all the time.

Genuine Sharing Charges Our Lives with Energy

My favorite example—and one that proves that sharing is inherent in human nature—is our inner need to return a favor when we receive something. Where does this need come from? According to the Kabbalists, this is known as "removing bread of shame." The complexity of this subject is studied in the first lessons in basic Kabbalah courses. To me, it was demonstrated thus: Imagine yourself in a strange city in the middle of the night, with no money and nowhere to sleep; suddenly you remember that your aunt, whom you hadn't seen or been in touch with for five years, lives there. In the middle of the night, you muster your courage and phone her (you have no other choice), and your aunt is overjoyed at the opportunity to welcome you to her home, shares her food with you, and sees to all your needs. How do you feel? Your conscience troubles you for having lost touch with her for so long and you immediately start thinking up ways to host her at your home, to return the favor. . . .

This need to return hospitality is natural. The moment we receive a gift, we immediately ask ourselves how we can reciprocate. For many people, the matter of sharing can become a problem—so used are they to giving that they have forgotten how to receive. This trait is known as excessive generosity and, like every excess, is problematic. If we want to achieve a naturally flowing and balanced energy, we must teach ourselves to receive as well as to share. Remember that by receiving, we actually allow and teach the other person to give.

Volunteering is one way of sharing unconditionally. However, volunteering to work as your "last job"—because you have too much time on your hands now that you are retired—will not fill you with the energy you require.

Since it is human nature to think in terms of profit and loss, you must learn to conduct the act of sharing voluntarily, on behalf of someone else, with no expectations of a reward. And yes, sometimes real sharing requires extra effort, but it has the ability to cause the kind of happiness and self-fulfillment that you are so in need of.

Here are a few examples: by unreservedly helping children overcome difficulties, you can change the world, since today's children are our future; volunteering to help in various institutions and welfare organizations; calling up someone you know is in need of some words of comfort and encouragement. There is no lack of people in need of your help. But remember, the idea of sharing is not only about handing out money; it is about giving of yourself.

How often should you volunteer? At least two hours a week.

The very act of sharing constitutes your own investment in health, and only when you experience it will you know what I am talking about. Your reward cannot be bought with money, anywhere in the world. It is the energy that will heal and protect you—the energy of caring for others.

Healing and Recovery

The various tools contained in this introduction constitute a kind of plan. When you implement this plan on a daily basis, a process takes place in your body both of healing and of immunization against disease.

What Is Spiritualism?

People always connect the term *spiritual* to religion, but I have no such intentions. You can be spiritual without being religious. Being spiritual means that you accept that there is another, higher, reason for the material world we are experiencing, for its reality. Being spiritual means not judging people, but understanding that the faults we see in others exist in us, too, so that it is not our place to sit in judgment of others, but of ourselves. Though people tend to think they are perfect and unmarred, they have been given the ability to see themselves and their behavior through the eyes of others (mirror effect), to understand and to better identify the issues and areas that require inner change. In other words, everything you don't like in others—exists in you, too.

Or, like attracts like. The frequency on which we exist and to which we are connected, whether it is positive or negative, attracts us to people who are exactly like ourselves. If you are in a good mood, the people you attract on that day are happy and cheerful, too; and if you leave home in a sad and depressed mood, you'll find that all the miseries in the world are gathered in your office. By the same principle, if you encounter an angry person, or two people quarrelling, this is a sign that similar situations exist in your own life and you must find out where. If you are angry with your husband or wife, and not getting along with them because they are different from you, or because their habits appear extreme, this means that you, too, possess a tiny percent of the same negative traits. Thus, complaining and whining to others is not the way to get them to change. Experience has taught me that it doesn't work.

Often, after a short argument, we wait, with all our pent-up anger, for the right moment to settle a score. The moment comes and we begin a conversation that had been cooking inside us for a long time. Words pour forth as if out of a pressure cooker, full of nervous anger, yet they fall on deaf ears and have no effect on the person before us. Even if that person appears completely attentive, inside, he or she wishes it were possible to escape this unpleasant situation. Your only achievement is that you've had your say! Apart from that, there's been no change and we find ourselves saying, "for twenty years, I've been saying the same thing, over and over again, and nothing happens."

You must understand that the minute the person under attack realizes the imminence of such a conversation, his aura (the electromagnetic field that surrounds him) closes and there is no chance of breaking through this armor. In my workshops, I compare this situation to a motorcyclist riding at top speed while mosquitoes and flies are crashing into his helmet, but are unable to touch him. The same applies to the words, the rockets and bombs that we release in a quarrel.

What Is the Correct Energy for Conducting a Conversation?

Before responding to something unpleasant that happened or was said to you, you would do well to wait at least three days (yes, it does sound like a long time). If, after three days, the entire content of the conversation is still echoing in your head, this is a sign that you should indeed talk about it. If you have forgotten what happened, it means that from the start, there was no need for your anger.

A conversation should be held peacefully, over a cup of coffee or tea, without the presence of children, saying simply what has to be said. Speak in a calm and pleasant tone and maintain it throughout the conversation. Remember that if you get angry, there will be no point to the conversation, because once again you will not achieve the expected results, a change in the situation.

You cannot change people; you can only help your significant other to want to be a better person.

The recognition that he or she has something that requires change or improvement from within has to come from him or her. You cannot force change on people. Try to remember the times you were ordered to go on a diet, to stop smoking, or anything else that required change. Your inner resistance was absolutely natural, because it is very hard for someone to hear that he or she is not perfect, even if he or she already knows it.

With this understanding and awareness, you should transfer the message to your partner. Find the best way to do so, and choose your words carefully, as if you were trying to pass on the message to yourself.

How Can You Achieve Crucial Change?

There exists a simple way to bring about swift and positive results: Refrain from saying to someone else what bothers you, and instead do some honest introspection, an examination of all aspects of your life, and find those moments and events when your behavior resembled similar behavior on the part of another. You could do the same with your children, relatives, or parents. Regardless of what you discover, your introspection should be conducted with an understanding that the moment you have managed to identify the flaw in yourself and you start working on repairing it, you will notice an automatic change in the attitude of others toward you. This formula is amazing; it always proves itself and it is my way of life. The repair can work with everyone you know, so include all the people with whom you are in daily contact: at work, home, extended family, etc.

Women reading this book should remember that, as a mother or wife, it is you who determine the energy in the home. If you are angry and bad-tempered, your husband and children will be the same. You have the ability to build or destroy your family's well-being; you should, therefore, choose a positive path and endeavor to be calm. Make a choice to do things that you find relaxing, that provide you with feelings of satisfaction and fulfillment.

Tools for Change

So far, everything mentioned in this section— the energy of water, water therapy, spiritual bathing, crystals, meditation and guided imagery—are spiritual tools that, together, have the power to help you achieve change wherever you choose. These tools actually create an energetic circle that supports and strengthens you in times of difficulty, when you want to change or upgrade your character traits. Without them, change is very hard to achieve.

Nothing in this book constitutes a substitute for conventional or alternative medicines and therapies that you are currently receiving or will receive in the future. This book provides you with support in all stages of the spiritual process you must undergo in order to become healthy and balanced.

Meditations for the Body

Shoulder Pain

Often the feeling that you carry the whole world on your shoulders expresses itself in chronic upper-back pain. Review the areas in which you feel yourself overburdened with responsibility. Ask yourself if you accepted these responsibilities willingly, and what you get out of having everything on your shoulders (e.g., does it allow you to control everyone in your vicinity or to enjoy the feeling of "no one can do without me?"). If you change your attitude toward responsibility and see it as something good and positive, and introduce a portion of genuine sharing into it, you will experience emotional relief and your shoulder pains will miraculously disappear. If you are burdening yourself with too much responsibility because you find it hard to delegate some of it to others (at home or at work), you must change this habit and learn to rely on others; otherwise you are harming your health.

I recommend doing a few simple shoulder exercises every day, taking up yoga, and trying some alternative therapies.

Suitable healing crystals: Amethyst, Malachite, Moonstone, Garnet, Fluorite

Meditation

Practice the correct breathing exercise at the beginning of the part "Meditations for the Soul."

Breathe deeply into your stomach and imagine a large ∞ on your shoulder.

Gaze at this mandala and imagine that the colors penetrate the pain through the ∞ and gradually seep inward.

At the same time, feel that you are exhaling the pain, the responsibility, and the burden.

Continue deep breathing like this for at least three minutes.

Close your eyes and imagine yourself in a different reality, one in which everyone is happy to help you to relieve you of your tasks, and to allow you to do things that you enjoy doing.

Count silently to ten and then open your eyes.

Headaches and Migraines

Begin each of these meditations with the correct breathing exercise at the beginning of the part "Meditations for the Soul."

Suitable healing crystals: Amethyst—cluster or crystal

Meditation

Breathe deeply as you focus on this mandala for two minutes. Imagine that the purple colors in the mandala are drawing your headache toward them.

Close your eyes and imagine your head emptying itself of all pain.

Remain like this for as long as you need to and then open your eyes.

Meditating with a Healing Crystal

Lay a small amethyst cluster or crystal on your forehead and imagine the crystal drawing out the pain.

Pressure and Massage Points

1. General head massage.
2. Locate and massage particularly painful points in your thumbs and toes.
3. Locate painful points in your shoulders and upper back, press firmly on them for half a minute, then release.
4. Lean your elbows on a table, turn your thumbs upward, and place them in the indent just below the eyebrows, at the inner corners, and lean your head forward. This position creates an upward pressure point.

Repeat the procedure several times. It hurts, but it is well worth it.

PMS—Premenstrual Syndrome

Meditation to renew the monthly menstrual cycle and alleviate pain.

It is worthwhile to practice all four stages at least once every day, rather than only during menstruation. The following exercises will balance the energy necessary for a regular menstrual cycle and enable you to heal yourself.

Suitable healing crystals: Carnelian, Moonstone, Garnet, Fluorite

Meditation

Practice the correct breathing exercise at the beginning of the part "Meditations for the Soul."

1. Stand with your legs spread wide, feet pointing out, with your back straight; bend your knees. With the help of your hip muscles, very slowly lower your buttocks as if planning to sit in a chair. When you reach the point of "sitting in a chair," return slowly to a standing position. Practice five of these "situps" twice a day.
2. Massage your entire ankle area; if you find a painful spot, massage it a little longer.
3. Sit in an armchair or on a sofa and place the outer part of your right foot on your left knee. Look for a prominent bone in your right ankle. Count a distance of six fingers from this bone in the direction of the knee (see illustration) and press this point with your thumb (vertical pressure). If this point is especially painful, you have reached the right place. Press as hard as you can tolerate and let go. Practice five repetitions of this massage three times a day. Each time you press on the point, the pain will lessen and your menstrual problems will be miraculously alleviated.
4. Lie on your back and rub your hands together. Imagine they are covered in orange color and lay them on your lower abdomen. Imagine the orange color being absorbed deep in your uterus, ovaries, and fallopian tubes.

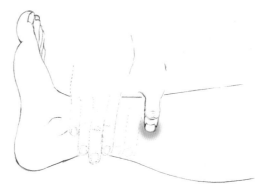

Tooth and Gum Pain

An Infusion of Healing Crystals

I suggest you purchase a large Blue Calcite or Fluorite crystal (at least the size of an egg) and prepare an infusion according to instructions in first chapter, Getting Started.

Drink at least three glasses of this infusion every day.

Drinking the infusion does not replace a visit to the dentist.

Meditation

Use the Kabbalistic healing at the beginning of the part "Meditations for the Soul."

Gaze at the combination of letters regarding the mouth (nos. 9 and 10 in the table), and imagine that the light and energy produced by these letter combinations change shape and burst in the form of light through your right palm.

Now hold your right hand over the painful area.

Another Recommendation

Press with your finger on the dent that is located between your upper lip and your nose. This is a pressure point that alleviates toothaches, gum aches, and releases stress in the jaws. Press for one minute and release. Repeat this several times.

General Pain

Suitable healing crystal: Amethyst cluster

Meditation

Sit comfortably and place the amethyst on the painful area. Imagine the crystal drawing out the pain. Imagine the pain flowing out through the healing crystal.

Close your eyes and breathe deeply for at least ten minutes.

Open your eyes and remove the crystal.

Now gaze at the colors of the mandala for at least three minutes as you breathe deeply.

Count to five and complete the meditation.

Another Meditation

Gaze at the colors of the mandala for at least three minutes while breathing deeply.

Now, take deep breaths and strongly exhale the pain five times.

Rub your hands together and lay them on the painful area.

Imagine the pain fading while you touch the place with your hands.

Continue breathing in this way for at least ten more breaths.

Now, take deep breaths into the center of the pain, and then exhale slowly and randomly, like the breathing sequence practiced in prenatal classes.

Repeat this breathing exercise five times.

Now gaze at the colors of the mandala and spread these colors through the center of the pain.

With every breath you take, feel the color alleviating the pain.

Do this for two minutes.

Close your eyes and illuminate your entire body with the color white.

Count up to ten in your heart and open your eyes.

Improved Facial Skin and a Youthful Appearance

I recommend a daily face wash with water that has had a Rose Quartz healing crystal immersed in it; I also suggest leaving a piece of Rose Quartz in a container of your favorite face cream.

Meditation

Practice the breathing exercise at the beginning of the part "Meditations for the Soul."

Breathe deeply and gaze at this mandala for at least two minutes.

Sit or lie comfortably on your back and focus your thoughts on your facial skin.

Rub your hands together and imagine that they are colored yellow; then lay them, fingers spread, on your face.

For at least one minute, imagine that the yellow color is being absorbed into every cell in your face.

You'll notice your wrinkles visibly reducing and your skin becoming clear, smooth, and uniform.

Remain with this thought for as long as you like.

You can rub your hands together and repeat the exercise several times.

Close your eyes and imagine the color pink wherever there was yellow previously.

See yourself looking younger, happier, and more relaxed. Everyone tells you that you are looking great.

Stay like this for at least two minutes.

Open your eyes and gaze at the mandala for as long as you like.

Beauty

Consider also using the previous meditation (Improved Facial Skin and a Youthful Appearance).

Suitable healing crystals: Rose Quartz—immersed in your drinking water and your moisturizing face cream

Meditation

Begin with the breathing exercise at the beginning of the part "Meditations for the Soul."

Gaze at this mandala.

Take deep breaths while thinking of the solar plexus in the middle of the abdomen.

Fill this energy center with the color yellow.

Imagine yourself surrounded by the colors yellow or gold.

With each breath you take, spread the color through your belly, legs, heart, hands, and head.

Now take ten deep breaths and think of your positive features. Ask in your heart to become and appear illuminated and positive.

Now gaze at the color pink in the mandala and love yourself.

Ask yourself to change and improve your features so as to always appear young looking.

Withdraw the color yellow/gold from yourself and your surroundings and imagine that you are pulling and raising the color toward your eyes, while taking five deep breaths.

Close your eyes for a moment, and imagine your inner beauty flowing out through your eyes to touch the entire world.

Open your eyes and smile.

Weight Loss: Meditative Support for a Diet

Choose a diet you find easy to follow.

Imagine how you would like to look at the end of the slimming process. See yourself clearly and in great detail with a new slim figure: in new clothes, with a different hairstyle, etc. If you have a photograph of yourself in a period of your life when you looked really good and you aspire to return to that look, keep it with this book, and look at it when you are practicing the meditation.

Suitable healing crystals: Apatite, Unakite, Green Tourmaline, Amethyst

Meditation

Begin with the breathing exercise at the beginning of the part "Meditations for the Soul."

Gaze at this mandala for at least one minute.

Inhale the colors deep into your stomach.

Exhale the way your current figure looks and bring out your new figure.

Decide that this time you will succeed.

Continue breathing for two more minutes and imagine that your new figure flatters you.

Focus on the colors of the mandala, imagining that they surround your stomach and intestines, and are improving your digestion process.

Continue breathing in this way for at least three minutes longer.

Now tighten your stomach so that you'll be satisfied with the diet you have chosen.

Close your eyes and imagine the color pink.

Spread it around your stomach and direct it from there to your entire digestive system.

Feel that the color pink is filling you with the energy of love, satisfaction, and contentment.

Count to seven and open your eyes.

Good luck!

Asthma and Breathing Difficulties

Feelings of suffocating and breathing difficulties are indicative of emotional suffocation, which results from a lack of freedom; whether from lack of expressing and realizing your personal potential, or from lack of freedom of speech (between husband and wife, in the workplace, etc.). In children, the sense of a lack of freedom could be the result of exaggerated control from their parents, strictness, or having too many restrictions. Children may also sense that their parents do not feel free to do what they want, or that the parents feel stuck in their own lives. If you or your child feels this way, I recommend avoiding spicy food and wearing red clothes. The colors green, turquoise, and blue are helpful in easing the breathing process.

Suitable healing crystals: Turquoise, Jade, Malachite, Amethyst, Moonstone, Pearl

Meditation

Gaze at the center of the mandala for a few minutes and breathe in and out at your own pace.

Imagine that the colors are flowing away from the page and into your lungs, expanding them.

Imagine that you are on vacation in a place that makes you feel relaxed, a place where you feel liberated, and allow peace and quiet to influence you.

With every breath you take, allow tranquility to enter your lungs and expand your chest cavity.

Continue breathing in this way for at least two minutes as you inhale the liberating colors of the mandala.

Now imagine that the colors of the mandala are reaching deep into your very soul and setting it free, as a sparrow is released from a tiny cage.

Continue breathing in this way for a full minute longer.

Imagine you are releasing your creative senses and your ability to fulfill dreams.

Now take a few longer and deeper breaths.

Close your eyes for a moment. Imagine that your body is entirely enveloped in the color turquoise and open your eyes when you feel ready.

Diabetes: Meditation to Lower Blood Sugar Levels

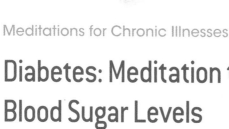

In order to achieve results, this meditation should be practiced at least twice a day. After your blood sugar levels have dropped and remain stable, continue practicing it at a regular hour only once daily. Measure your blood sugar levels immediately after practicing the meditation.

Consult with your doctor with regard to reducing your medication. Do not discontinue or reduce your medication without medical consultation!

This meditation has been tried on volunteers and their medications were reduced fourfold after four weeks of daily practice. In addition, I strongly recommend trying the water therapy described in the first chapter, Getting Started. The pancreas—the organ responsible for regulating blood sugar—is located in the upper abdomen between the stomach and the spine. I suggest you find a picture of the pancreas and keep it with this book. This way you will be able to easily imagine the whole process.

Suitable healing crystals: Citrine, Serpentine, Chrysocolla

Meditation

Practice the breathing exercises at the beginning of the part "Meditations for the Soul."

Gaze at the center of this mandala for two minutes. Inhale the color yellow deep into your pancreas and imagine the color being absorbed and causing the pancreas to return to its normal function.

Take ten deep breaths as you imagine it filling with insulin, using an imaginary tap from which you release the amount of insulin necessary for your body.

The insulin now causes a drop in your blood sugar level. Imagine the balanced results showing on your diabetes monitor. Continue breathing with this thought in mind while gazing at the mandala. Decide that your blood sugar level is balancing itself and is staying stable.

Continue breathing with this thought in mind while gazing at the mandala.

Now close your eyes and think of the color purple.

Color your pancreas purple, take ten deep, relaxed breaths, and open your eyes.

Ulcers and Irritable Bowel Syndrome (IBS): Meditation for Relieving Heartburn and Stomach Pains

In order to completely solve your digestive and stomach problems, you might consider a fundamental change in your eating habits and food combinations. The diet described in *Fit for Life*, has proved itself effective among dozens of my patients who suffered from various intestinal problems. Indeed, within a week on the diet, their issues were solved.

The water therapy described in the first chapter, Getting Started, could also be of great help.

Suitable healing crystals: An infusion of Rose Quartz and/or Serpentine

Meditation

Practice the breathing exercise at the beginning of the part "Meditations for the Soul."

Gaze at the center of the mandala and breathe deeply for at least two minutes.

Rub your hands together and imagine they are being covered with the color pink.

Rest your hands over your stomach.

Imagine the color pink seeping down into your stomach and curing it.

Hold this thought and breathe deeply for three minutes.

Imagine the acidity level in your stomach decreasing and feel your stomach relaxing.

Imagine yourself eating more slowly, chewing your food thoroughly before swallowing it. Promise your body that you will practice this meditation regularly.

Continue breathing deeply into your stomach, maintaining the energy of the color pink.

Close your eyes and allow yourself to be more relaxed and peaceful and decide to change.

Release your hands, count backward from ten to one, and open your eyes.

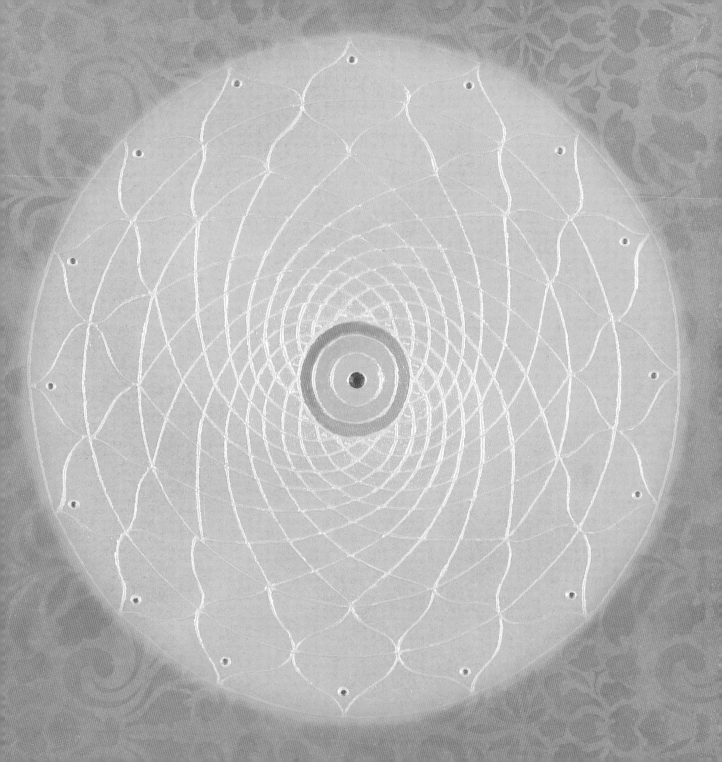

Heart: Meditation to Alleviate Chest Pains and Postoperative Stress

You hear the expression "don't take it to heart," which you should heed in this meditation, often. But how do you achieve it? How do you stop "taking things to heart"?

Here are a few pointers to introspection that may strengthen you:

- When you take things to heart, you are harming your health.
- Each time you take something to heart, try instead to replace it with a positive thought. For example, if a deal has fallen through, you could think, "I know I can't see the whole picture and that everything will change for the best." If you are hurt by someone, ask yourself, "Does this warrant feeling insulted? Perhaps it can be talked over with the person who hurt me?" You'll often find that he or she has no idea what you are talking about.
- Ask yourself, "What can I learn from this about myself? Do I also hurt others? Am I sensitive enough to those around me?"

Honest replies to these questions and a change of behavior on your part will lower your vulnerability and you'll soon see that you are no longer susceptible to insult.

Suitable healing crystals: Aventurine, Rose Quartz, Malachite, Chrysocolla, Turquoise, Jade

Meditation

With the next breath you take, let the colors enter your throat, your chest cavity, and your heart. From there, they will flow into the rest of your body via your bloodstream.

Your heart, which is located at the center of the flow, is now flooded with colors that nourish it and help it to overcome all situations.

Gaze at the mandala, take two deep breaths, and feel the colors soaking into your heart.

Close your eyes, feel the colors balance you, and allow positive energy and healing to flow into your heart.

Hold this position for at least three minutes more and open your eyes.

Hypertension: Meditation for Lowering Blood Pressure

This meditation is appropriate in cases when high blood pressure is the result of problems in the arteries. Practice it at least three times daily. I also suggest changing your diet, in accordance with professional advice.

In order to raise low blood pressure, you should practice meditations that relate to the color red.

Suitable healing crystals: Serpentine, Hematite, Bloodstone, Chrysocholla

Meditation

Practice the breathing exercise at the beginning of the part "Meditations for the Soul."

Gaze at this mandala and breathe deeply for two minutes.

Now, think of the arteries and veins in your body and imagine them as blocked pipes.

Open and release these blocks in any way you think appropriate (some suggestions: water flow, a bulldozer, a mallet, the colors of the mandala) and watch the blood flow easily through your arteries and veins.

Know that your high blood pressure is becoming balanced and settled.

Hold this thought as you take twenty more deep and relaxed breaths, while gazing at the mandala.

Decide that even when you are stressed or undergoing change, there will be no change in your balanced blood pressure.

Close your eyes and ask for positive thoughts that will have a beneficial effect on your health to become a part of your daily routine.

Take five deep breaths into your stomach and open your eyes.

Constipation: Relieving Chronic and Temporary Constipation

Suitable healing crystals: Jasper, Pyrite, Citrine, Tiger's Eye

Constipation is a symptom of repression and lack of liberty, both of the body and of the soul. The following are self-help exercises; I suggest you try them all before settling on the one most suitable for you. You can also combine several of them simultaneously.

1. Adopt the "water therapy" explained in the first chapter, Getting Started.
2. As you are still lying in bed in the morning, drink a glass of cool water and then, using circular movements with your thumb, massage the spot that is located one centimeter above your navel (in a direct line toward the throat).
3. While sitting on the toilet, avoid placing pressure on your intestines (which causes hemorrhoids); rather, sit patiently and imagine your intestines filling with a white light, which is moving and pushing the feces gently down toward the anus.
4. Lay your hands on your belly and drag them around in circular, clockwise movements, placing slight pressure, from the top of the stomach, to the left, downward, then back to the top from the right side. Imagine this movement activating the intestines to be rid of the feces.
5. For a spiritual treatment: Lie on your back and relax your muscles in any way that is comfortable to you. Think of the things that hold you back in your life. Choose one of them and image yourself pushing it out through an imaginary hole in your lower back toward the ground. Once you feel that you have indeed released that troubling issue, you can move on to the next one.
6. If you are constipated because you are dissatisfied with your body, or because you feel repressed and unable to let yourself go, you might consider joining a belly-dancing class, a yoga class, or a laughter therapy workshop. Try it and see!
7. Meditation: Imagine yourself flying above the sea and releasing into it all the emotional waste that has accumulated in your heart and in your intestines. Watch it dropping into the sea and disappearing. Repeat this meditation at least twice a week.
8. Introduce changes to your diet.

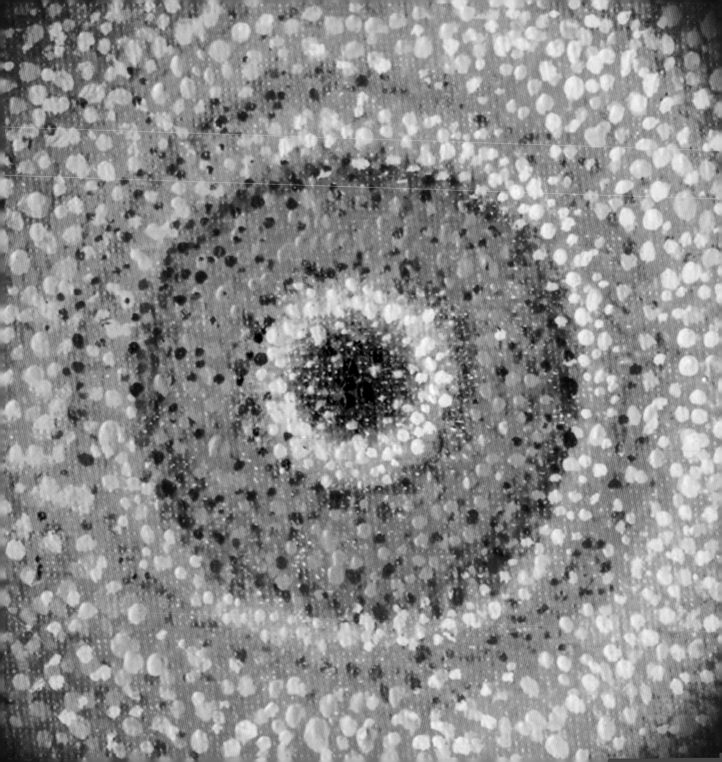

Fatigue

If you are troubled by chronic fatigue, the solution is to do something strenuous when you are at your most tired, because creative activity fills the body with renewed energy. In order to take the first step, even if you feel at this moment that it is impossible, you should practice this meditation every morning and whenever you feel overcome with fatigue.

I also recommended adopting the "water therapy" explained in the first chapter, Getting Started.

This meditation is not suitable for people who suffer from high blood pressure, heart problems, or cancer. It should not be practiced before sleep.

Suitable healing crystals: Carnelian (infused in water), Ox's Eye (Red Tiger's Eye), Copper, Red Jasper

Meditation

Sit in a straight-backed chair (not one you can rest back in comfortably).

Feel your feet resting on the floor.

Feel the connection with the earth.

Focus on the vertebrae in your lower back (tailbone, sacrum) and imagine them painted in orange light.

Allow the orange-red color to spill over and color your legs and feet.

Allow the orange-red color to rise and fall, rise and fall, up and down along the length of your spine and legs.

These colors awaken and invigorate you.

Stay surrounded by these colors for as long as you can.

Before deciding to stop the exercise, close your eyes and color your body with a blue light.

Count to ten and then open your eyes.

Colds and Throat Infections

A chronic throat infection is indicative of improper use of your "right to speak," or the ability of self-expression, which is given to you in order to express your thoughts and feelings. Improper use is often manifested in not expressing feelings and refraining from talking about things that bother you, or in talking too much and not choosing your words wisely. This causes an energy imbalance in the center of your throat and can eventually even lead to difficulties in swallowing —a feeling of having something stuck in your throat that you can't release, rather like the feeling you get when you are about to cry. If this is how you feel, let yourself go and cry. There is nothing shameful in crying! Crying, if you are unused to it, has the ability to release tension in the area of the throat energy center.

In addition to this meditation, I recommend you practice the meditations for Reinforcing Your Immune System and Stuttering and Speech Impediments.

Suitable healing crystals: Blue Lace Agate, Turquoise, Blue Calcite, Kynite, Lapis

Meditation

Gaze at the center of the mandala and breathe deeply for one minute.

Create a bubble around you made up of the colors in the mandala.

With each breath you take, inhale the colors through your mouth, your nose (if it is blocked, rub the bridge and both nostrils), and via the throat into your lungs.

Allow the colors to soak into your nose tunnels, throat, tonsils, and vocal cords.

With each exhalation, release your emotional burdens and all those things that you find hard to talk about.

Imagine the mucus and phlegm drying and your body overcoming the infection.

Exhale all the pain out of your body. Continue until you feel relief.

For a moment, brush with red all those places that were previously colored sky blue.

Close your eyes and imagine that you are healthy and happy. Count to ten and open your eyes.

Postoperative Recovery

Suitable healing crystals: Chrysocolla, Rose Quartz—you can prepare an infusion from these healing crystals and lay poultices of this infusion over the scar, in order for the incision to heal.

Meditation

Gaze at the colors of the mandala on the opposite page as you take ten deep breaths. Now breathe deeply and draw the colors toward the location of the operation.

Imagine the area soaking in the colors and using them for inner healing.

Breathe in this way for as many times as you need.

Close your eyes and imagine the scar healing quickly and disappearing, and imagine you are functioning as usual, and healing miraculously.

Open your eyes.

Now rub your hands together and lay them over the location of the operation.

Feel a healing energy passing through the palms of your hands.

Breathe in this way at least ten times, then relax your hands.

Cold Feet

In order to warm up cold feet and to improve blood circulation, I recommend a hot shower that you should end with a burst of cold water. I also recommend reading the paragraph about spiritual immersing in the first chapter, Getting Started, and doing some kind of physical activity (walking, jogging, bicycling).

Suitable healing crystals: Ruby, Red Jasper, Carnelian, Hematite

Meditation

Gaze at the center of this mandala and fill your feet with its colors (you can imagine this as far up as your knees).

Take deep breaths for at least one minute as you color your feet red.

Take deep breaths into your abdomen, and in your mind, allow your breath to flow into your feet, as if your lungs can stretch that far.

Concentrate on your feet and feel your breathing flow through your toes.

Continue breathing in this way for at least three minutes longer.

Close your eyes and think of the color turquoise.

For a moment, color all the places that were previously flooded with red, in turquoise. Count down silently from ten to one and move your toes for about one minute.

Feel that your feet are now warm and open your eyes.

Self-Healing

Green is a color that raises the level of your body's immune system, so you might like to practice this meditation when you catch a cold or feel sick.

Cancer patients should exchange the color green for deep pink or turquoise and might like to be helped by my book, *Therefore Choose Life*.

Suitable healing crystals: Azurite, Amethyst, Emerald, Green Tourmaline

Meditation

Practice the breathing exercise at the beginning of the part "Meditations for the Soul."

Gaze at the center of this mandala for at least three minutes.

Imagine the colors entering your heart and, from there, making their way to your back.

Your spine is colored from top to bottom.

Think of balance in every sphere of your life and take ten deep breaths, during which you distribute the colors throughout your body.

If you are also in need of the power of healing, focus on the color green and hold it for a while longer.

Now exhale and distribute the colors throughout your aura.

Close your eyes and lay your hands on the area in your body that needs healing.

Hold this position for as long as you want.

Count to ten and open your eyes.

Alleviating Nausea

Suitable healing crystals: Rose Quartz, Citrine, Turquoise, Tourmaline

Meditation

Gaze at the mandala and take ten deep breaths into your stomach.

Now open your left hand and lay the fingers of your right hand on your left forearm (see illustration).

With your thumb, press on the pressure point (the purple point in the illustration).

Hold this position as you breathe three times and release.

Press again, breathe three times, and release.

Repeat this exercise five consecutive times.

Now follow the same sequence on your right forearm and press it with your left thumb.

After completing the exercise, close your eyes for a moment, think of the color pink, count to ten, and open your eyes.

Deep Sleep

The ability to fall asleep easily, to sleep deeply, and to awaken full of energy in the morning depends on several factors, the most important of which is your activity during the day and the energies to which you choose to connect. If you decide to be as active as possible (rather than bored), to fill yourself with love (rather than with nervousness and anger), to share (rather than to take), and to care for others (rather than to think only of yourself), you will fulfill your potential and feel happy and satisfied with your life. This kind of lifestyle provides nourishment for the soul within you, and can change and determine the quality of your sleep.

Suitable healing crystals: Lepidolite, Amethyst, Sodalite, Mica, Green Tourmaline, Lapis

Meditation

Gaze for at least two minutes at the center of this mandala.

Start practicing the breathing exercise at the beginning of the part "Meditations for the Soul."

With closed eyes, squint toward the topmost point on the bridge of your nose.

Take five relaxed breaths in this position and relax your eyes, so that they are in their normal state.

Rub your hands together and lay the palms of your hands lightly over your closed eyes without touching your eyelashes.

Exhale and inhale calmly for a count of twenty.

You will feel pleasant warmth interacting between your eyes and your hands.

You may rub your hands together and repeat the exercise several times more.

Count to four and remove your hands from your eyes.

Close your eyes and examine the day that has just passed; feel thankful for what you have.

Hold this thought and take several deep breaths for at least one minute.

Open your eyes and gaze for as long as you like at this mandala.

Reinforcing Your Immune System

Your thymus gland is located in the center of your chest, in a straight line between your heart and your throat. This gland is responsible for, among other things, the body's growth process and, according to conventional medicine, it shrinks with age until it becomes indistinguishable from surrounding fatty tissue. According to alternative medicine, it continues to function and contains within it the energy of the immune system.

Note: This meditation is also suitable for AIDS patients.

Cancer patients should imagine the color deep pink instead of green. They can also be helped by the book *Therefore Choose Life*.

Suitable healing crystals: Pink Tourmaline, Rutilated Quartz, Jade, Lapis, Malachite

Meditation

Form your hands into fists and drum on your thymus gland in the middle of your chest (like King Kong), for at least one minute as you think about awakening your immune system and its functions.

Gaze at this mandala, imagine its colors enveloping you, and with your breath, inhale them into your chest via this gland.

Take another ten deep breaths like these.

Imagine the gland absorbing the colors, which influence the entire chest cavity, especially the heart and lungs.

Close your eyes and imagine the color green flowing in and reaching your lymph nodes and reinforcing them (in your armpits, at either side of your throat, and in your groin).

See yourself as stronger and immune to all illness.

Count to seven and open your eyes.

Diarrhea

Suitable healing crystals: Golden Tiger's Eye, Citrine, Yellow Jasper, Chrysocolla

Meditation

Rub your hands together and lay them on your abdomen.

Practice the breathing exercise at the beginning of the part "Meditations for the Soul."

Rub your hands together once again, lay them on your abdomen, and massage your stomach in a circular, anticlockwise motion, at least ten times.

In your mind, stop the movement of your intestines and your diarrhea.

Place your right thumb on your navel and press down gently (no more deeply than one centimeter).

Imagine that through your navel, you are transferring healing powers down into your intestines and stopping your diarrhea.

Hold this position for at least two minutes.

Rub your hands together and lay them on your stomach as you take ten more deep breaths.

Inhale the colors of the mandala on the opposite page into your stomach.

Remove your hands and shake them two or three times.

Open your eyes.

Meditations for the Soul

Instructions for Correct Breathing

Good, deep, relaxed breathing allows energy to flow into your soul. When your soul is fulfilled, your body is healthy. In other words, breathing prepares a suitable foundation for healing. The source of correct breathing can be found in yoga and many books on yoga offer various styles of breathing.

I have chosen to show you the simplest and most comfortable one. You can practice it lying down or sitting up. If you are unfamiliar with the phrase "breathe into your belly," and have never practiced it, please do this first (lying down and resting your hands on your abdomen, near the navel): Focus your thoughts on your navel, imagine that you are breathing into it and feel that you are inflating it as you inhale. Exhale and empty the stomach cavity of air.

Keep your breathing as slow and relaxed as you can. If you are lying on your back as you practice this breathing, with your hands on your abdomen, feel your palms rising. Repeat this inhaling and exhaling exercise at least ten consecutive times.

Now inhale into your navel to a count of four. When you reach four, start exhaling to the count of four, at the same rhythm you used while inhaling. Repeat twenty times. And now for an additional option: After filling your abdomen with air and when you have reached a count of four, stop breathing, count to four, and exhale all the air. Repeat this ten times. Finally, take another twenty breaths to the rhythm of four, only inhaling and exhaling (without holding your breath).

I suggest you practice breathing while gazing at the mandala.

How many times a day should I practice breathing?

Try breathing correctly at least twice a day and preferably before going to sleep. The idea is to breathe like this at every opportunity, even if you weren't planning to practice, e.g., while driving, cooking, taking a shower, or watching TV.

Additions to breathing exercises to increase your ability to heal yourself:

Imagine that you are inside a bubble of light and that you are inhaling the light, letting it spread throughout your body.

Try to remember this exercise by heart, since it appears at the beginning of every meditation.

Kabbalistic Healing

Technology for the Soul

Most schools of self-awareness contain similar ways of thinking: think positively, be happy, value what you have, accept with love everything that happens in your life, control your anger, and love everyone equally (love thy neighbor), as in unconditional love.

Examine this short list, which is aimed at turning your life into a tranquil and happy one. But is it really so simple and quick to fulfill even one of the things on this list?

Experience has shown that a decision to bring about inner change (even in the wake of a powerful event in one's life) is not so easy to fulfill. Indeed, in the next test you face, you likely won't be able to maintain the cool façade you promised yourself.

I have always liked the idea of being permanently happy, but the ability to stick to it even in times of hardship is something else altogether. It is here that the table of the 72 Names of God letter combinations can help you. Just gazing at the letter combination you choose to meditate on, while taking deep breaths and directing your thinking, will bring about miracles in your life and affect your ability to change your life. I personally make use of these letters with regard to all kinds of issues, every minute of my life. Without this table, I wouldn't be where I am today. And all this from simply looking and focusing your thoughts! It's well worth trying.

Each of the combinations in this table draws a different kind of energy to your life. Following are a number of useful examples: ללה (first row) helps provide deeper sleep and genuine dreams; הקם (second row) draws out depression; סאל (sixth row) increases energy for wealth and prosperity; פוי (seventh row) erases anger; מנד (fifth row) eliminates fear; and עמם (seventh row) introduces excitement to your life.

This table encompasses all areas of your life and helps you control your feelings and various character traits (you can find explanations for all the letter combinations in the table in Yehuda Berg's bestselling book, *72 Names of God*).

וְהוּ	יְלִי	סִיט	עֵלְם	מַהֵשׁ	לֵלַה	אָכָא	כֵּהֵת
הֵזִי	אֶלֶד	לָאו	הָהַע	יָזֵל	מֵבַה	הֵרִי	הֵקֵם
לְאו	כָּלִי	לֵוו	פָּהֵל	נֶלֵך	יִיי	מֵלֵה	וֵזֵהוּ
נְתַה	הָאָא	יֵרֵת	שְׁאָה	רִיי	אוּם	לֵכָב	וְשֵׁר
יְוֵזו	לֵהוו	כוק	מֶנָד	אָנִי	וְזַעֵם	רֵהֵע	יִיז
הֵהֵה	מִיכ	ווֹל	יְלָה	סָאל	עֵרִי	עָשֵׁל	מִיה
וְהוּ	דָנִי	הוֹשׁ	עֵמַם	נֵנָא	נִית	מֵבַה	פוִי
נֵמַם	יִיל	הַרוּ	מַצֵר	וֵמֵב	יֵהֵה	עֵנוּ	מוֹזִי
דֵמֵב	מֵנָק	אִיע	וֵזֵבוּ	רָאה	יֵבֵמ	הַיִי	מוּם

Healing for the Soul

This table, the Tikkun HaNefesh, is a very powerful Kabbalistic healing tool. It combines with the Kabbalistic meditation, Ana Be'Ko'ach, but it can also be used on its own.

How Is It Done?

You gaze at the letter combinations and, with your right hand, you pass the energy to whichever spot you wish while imagining a healing light leaving the palm of your hand toward the organ you are healing. You pass over the organs according to the order of the numbers in the table. For example: You gaze only at the letter combination י-ה-ו-ה "Keter—skull" (no. 1 in the table) and, using a slow movement, pass your hand from the top of your head forward to the forehead and back toward your neck. Each combination affects different areas in your body, according to details in the table. You can stay as long as you wish and heal those organs that are in more need of intense help.

Healing for Organs According to the Table of Tikkun HaNefesh

1. The center part of the head, from the forehead to the nape of the neck.
2. The right side of the head, from the right temple to the base of the skull.
3. The left side of the head, from the left temple to the base of the skull.
4. The right eye.
5. The left eye.
6. The right ear.
7. The left ear.
8. The right nostril.
9. The left nostril.
10. The mouth.
11. The parts of the mouth:
    The throat - אחה"ע
    The palate - גיכ"ק
    The tongue - דטלנ"ת
    The teeth - זסשר"ץ
    The lips - בומ"ף
12. The right arm.
13. The left arm.
14. The body—all the organs from the base of the neck down to the lower abdomen, including the internal organs (the heart, the kidneys, the liver, the pancreas, the intestines, etc.).
15. The right leg.
16. The left leg.
17. The masculine and feminine reproductive organs and the spine.
18. The feet.

3
LEFT BRAIN מוח שמאל
BINAH בינה
יֱהֱוֱהּ

1
גלגלתא SKULL
KETER כתר
יַהֲוָהּ

2
מוח ימין RIGHT BRAIN
CHOCHMA חכמה
יַהֲוַהּ

5
עין שמאל LEFT EYE
יהוה יהוה
יהוה
יהוה יהוה

9 8
חוטם NOSE

4
עין ימין RIGHT EYE
יהוה יהוה
יהוה
יהוה יהוה

7
אזן שמאל LEFT EAR
יוד הי ואו הה

6
אזן ימין RIGHT EAR
יוד הי ואו הה

10
פה MOUTH
יוד הי **11**ואו הי
אחה"ע גיכ"ק דטלנ"ת
זסשר"ץ בומ"ף

13
זרוע שמאל LEFT ARM
GEVURAH גבורה
יְהֹוָה

14
גוף BODY
TIFERET תפארת
יֱהֹוָה

12
זרוע ימין RIGHT ARM
CHESED חסד
יֵהֵוֵהּ

16
ירך שמאל LEFT LEG
HOD הוד
יְהֹוָה

17
REPRODUCTIVE ORGANS
YESOD יסוד
יו הו וו הו

15
ירך ימין RIGHT LEG
NETZACH נצח
יְהֹוָה

18
רגל FEET
עטרה
MALCHUT מלכות
יהואדנהי

Relaxing in a Pasture

Meditation

Begin with the breathing exercise at the beginning of the part "Meditations for the Soul," practicing it twice in a row.

Gaze at the colors of this mandala and breathe deeply for at least two minutes.

Imagine that you are in a green field that spreads out toward the horizon.

The earth is soft and fertile.

Some distance from you, there is a lone tree and you approach it.

The earth is especially soft and you dig a pit with great ease.

When the pit is deep enough, you can throw into it all those things that burdened you today,

last week,

last year,

and altogether.

Feel that you are unburdening your shoulders, your arms, your heart, your stomach, and, especially, your head.

Continue emptying yourself until you feel relief.

Now use the soft earth to cover all those things you threw into the pit.

You can always return here to practice the meditation or, if you need to, you can return to take back your things.

Close your eyes for a moment, breathe deeply for a full minute, and feel the relief.

Count to four and open your eyes.

Relaxing by Connecting to Nature

Look for a tree in the vicinity of your home.

The tree can be growing next to your window, in your garden, or in the yard across the road.

Position yourself so that you can see the tree clearly and make yourself comfortable.

Tip: If the tree is in your own yard, lie down under it, weather permitting.

Meditation

Practice the breathing exercise at the beginning of the part "Meditations for the Soul," practicing it twice in a row.

Focus on the color green and the movement of the leaves, listen to the whisper of the leaves in the wind, and connect to this tranquility.

With each breath you take, inhale serenity into yourself.

Allow the tree to calm you, by itself, by its own movement, with the green and the sky in the background.

Hold this for as long as it is pleasant, as you inhale deeply.

Close your eyes and imagine your tomorrow to be full of joy.

Take five more deep breaths and open your eyes.

Releasing Emotional Stress

Meditation

Begin with the breathing exercise at the beginning of the part "Meditations for the Soul," practicing it twice in a row.

Gaze at the mandala for at least two minutes. Imagine ten stairs in front of you. Go up the steps until you reach a door. Open the door and enter a pink room. Stand in the center of the room and feel the pink softening and relaxing you. In the pink room, you'll leave behind all the troubles you've experienced over the past week. You can stay in the pink room for as long as you feel is necessary.

Leave the room. Go up another ten steps and enter an orange room. Soak in the orange color from the room's walls. Here, you'll leave behind all the unpleasant experiences of the last year, all the while filling yourself with the orange color. Remain here for as long as you feel the need.

Leave the orange room and climb another ten steps. You'll then find yourself in the center of a room painted turquoise. Inhale the color turquoise and feel liberated and weightless. In this room, you'll leave behind all the unpleasant experiences of your childhood, your adolescence, your teen years, and whenever else.

Turquoise can cope with anything and you are emptying everything into it. Stay in this room for as long as you need.

You are so light now that you can float up ten more steps and enter a white room.

This room is sparkling in its whiteness and you are light and clean and soaking up all the whiteness into each and every one of your cells, and into your entire body. You are floating in this room as if in a dream.

Stay in this room for as long as you need and just fill yourself up with light.

Close your eyes and count to ten.

Open your eyes and ask your heart to allow this good feeling to stay with you for as long as possible.

Wriggle your feet, toes, and fingers; breathe deeply into your stomach and release.

Muscle Relaxation and Deep Sleep

Prepare a positive thought that you can use at the end of this meditation.

Suitable healing crystals: Fluorite, Amethyst, Sugilite, Sodalite, Aventurine, Aquamarine, Rose Quartz, Tourmaline

Meditation

Lie on your back and relax your head and back of your neck.

Gaze at the center of this mandala for at least two minutes.

Practice two rounds of the breathing exercise at the beginning of the part "Meditations for the Soul."

Now relax your vertebrae one by one down to your shoulders and feel yourself sinking into the pillow/mattress on which you are lying.

Let go of your stubbornness.

Now relax your shoulder muscles.

Relax your arms right down to your fingertips.

Exhale the feeling that you are giving more than you are receiving.

Relax your chest cavity and breathe out everything that is troubling you.

Relax your abdomen and internal organs.

Relax your pelvis and legs.

Relax your feet.

Close your eyes and think one positive thought (the one you prepared in advance).

Take five deep breaths and sink into a sweet sleep.

Balance of the Body and Soul

Careful maintenance of your body's energetic balance can provide you with long-term inner peace and quiet. This meditation helps maintain this balance and also develops a fine connection with the body's needs; it also teaches you to listen to your body.

Meditation

Begin with the breathing exercise at the beginning of the part "Meditations for the Soul."

Continue with deep breathing and gazing at the colors of the mandala for at least two minutes.

Imagine the colors entering your heart, moving from there to your back, and painting your spine from top to bottom.

Close your eyes for a moment and wish to be as balanced as possible in every way.

Take ten deep breaths, during which you will distribute the colors throughout your body.

Remain like this for at least three minutes.

Think of the places in your body that you wish to balance. Send a generous quantity of the mandala's colors to these parts, and watch as the colors are absorbed.

Now look down at your body in a view from above.

See the colors of your body and notice those parts in which the colors appear darker.

Breathe deeply into those parts until the colors become lighter.

Now close your eyes. Imagine white color enveloping you and hold this thought for at least two minutes.

Count to ten and open your eyes.

Cleansing the Aura

If you feel in need of spiritual cleansing, read the paragraph relating to it in the first chapter, Getting Started.

Suitable healing crystals: Botswana Agate, Quartz

Meditation

Practice the breathing exercise at the beginning of the part "Meditations for the Soul."

Gaze at this mandala, while taking ten deep breaths.

Imagine yourself surrounded by rings of fire:

One around your head,

One around your throat,

One around your heart,

One around your abdomen,

One around your knees, and

One around your feet.

The fire is drawing out all the negative energy and the color black that is in your aura.

Imagine the fire thoroughly cleansing the aura and clearing your awareness.

Close your eyes and see where the fire is still burning.

Extinguish the rings of fire in those places where the black color has receded and continue waiting until all the colors around you become clearer and brighter.

Extinguish the remaining rings of fire and imagine that all the colors of the rainbow are dancing around you.

Stay within the dance of color for as long as you want.

When you choose to re-emerge, count to ten and open your eyes.

Positive Thinking: Meditation for Enlightened Thought Process

Negative or positive thoughts have the ability to determine the reality in which you live; it is therefore better to think only positive thoughts, as this is a sure way to improve the reality that surrounds you.

How can you achieve this? Practice the following meditation. If you wish for answers that are more profound and based on your own life experience, you might like to study Kabbalah, or healing, or read Rhonda Byrne's *The Secret*.

Suitable healing crystals: Amethyst, Sodalite, Lapis, Chalcedony, Fluorite

Meditation

In order to halt your current negative thought waves, close your eyes and squint toward the topmost point on the bridge of your nose.

Hold this position as you take at least five deep breaths. Release and open your eyes.

Continue by practicing the breathing exercise at the beginning of the part "Meditations for the Soul."

Imagine yourself traveling through your head until you reach your thought reservoir.

Gaze at the center of the mandala for at least four minutes while filling your thought reservoir with these colors.

Now close your eyes and imagine that you are surrounded by every possible shade of the color orange.

Fill your thought reservoir with orange, with vitality, with positive attitude and joy.

Count to seven silently and open your eyes.

Intuition: Reinforcing Your Spiritual Vision

This meditation contains an instruction for receiving messages. It will connect you to your Sixth Sense and your gut feeling and help you develop them. When your energies are connected to positive frequencies, you will be able to receive positive messages. Whenever you want to receive real answers and messages, you should make the choice to be connected to positive frequencies.

This meditation mentions the pituitary gland that is located at the top front of your head. A precise description of this gland's function is not necessary in order to meditate successfully.

Suitable healing crystals: as you meditate, either place a Fluorite or an Amethyst crystal on your forehead, or you can hold in your hand a Citrine, a Cat's Eye, or a Sapphire crystal

Meditation

Gaze at the center of this mandala for at least three minutes.

Practice the breathing exercise at the beginning of the part "Meditations for the Soul."

Return to gaze at the mandala and imagine the colors entering your head through the center of your forehead.

Continue this until your head is completely full of the colors blue and purple.

Ask for the colors to surround your head and become absorbed into your pituitary gland.

Now, create a dense cloud of blue and purple and let it surround your head.

Continue breathing deeply for three minutes.

Close your eyes and connect to the energy of positive thoughts and spiritual messages.

Ask to be given the message you need.

Wait a few minutes longer and, if you don't get a message, try again another time (never give up!).

Spread a golden net over the colorful cloud that surrounds your head and ask for this energy to be maintained for as long as possible.

Take five deep breaths and open your eyes.

Loving Yourself: Meditation with Healing Crystals

In order to give love to someone else, you must first love yourself—when you love yourself, you'll have something genuine to give others. This meditation rejoins the heart and heals it (from a physical point of view, too), increases your self-confidence, and creates a basis for unconditional love.

Suitable healing crystals: Chrysocolla, Rose Quartz, Tiger's Eye, Blue Lace Agate

Meditation

Place the healing crystal of your choice in the center of your chest (preferably directly on your skin).

Imagine that the area on which the crystal lies contains an energy opening through which you can breathe directly into your heart. Now take deep and relaxed breaths through it.

Imagine the crystal expanding your heart while at the same time drawing into itself everything that is troubling you.

Keep breathing this way until you feel relief.

Lay your right hand on top of the healing crystal and place your left hand on top of your right hand.

Imagine a vital energy reflecting from your right hand to your left.

The energy is flowing in circles from your right hand to your left, through your shoulders and nourishes your heart with life.

Close your eyes, hold this thought, and then breathe for as long as you like.

Count to five and open your eyes.

Remove the crystal from your chest and rinse it in flowing water.

Attracting Your Soul Mate

Prepare a list of the physical and personality traits you are seeking in your soul mate. Examine this list and compare it with your own physical and personality traits. Note: Your list must contain almost identical qualities to those of the partner you are seeking (otherwise, I and this meditation will be unable to help you).

The ability to attract a partner is based on the theory of "like attracts like," so that if you want to get a better life partner, you should first raise the level of your own qualities.

Suggestions for the character traits in your checklist should include: honesty, integrity, open-mindedness, unconditional love, willingness to commit, ambition to succeed—in other words, perfection.

Note: This meditation will be helpful if you are emotionally free to take on a new love. Don't use it with regard to past relationships, because it will spoil your chances of receiving your real soul mate.

Suitable healing crystals: Rose Quartz, Moonstone, Peridot

Meditation

Begin with the breathing exercise at the beginning of the part "Meditations for the Soul."

Gaze at the center of this mandala for at least two minutes.

Breathe the colors deep into your heart for another minute.

Imagine a bubble of light, inside of which is the image of your soul mate (the image is usually quite blurred; if you are fortunate, you might get a clear picture of his/her face).

Imagine his/her character traits and abilities.

Imagine an arc of light and color passing from the image and into your heart.

Hold this thought for two minutes.

Close your eyes and imagine your life once love has entered it.

Imagine yourself married and a parent to children and always in love.

Count to three silently and open your eyes.

Anniversaries and Valentine's Day

A perfect marital partnership requires a lot of work; if you are happy to invest in your partnership, your life will be full of joy and fulfillment.

This meditation is best practiced together with your partner, lying down on your backs. You can hold hands.

This meditation can also be practiced on Valentine's Day.

Suitable healing crystals: Rose Quartz, Moonstone, Peridot

Meditation

Take deep breaths into your stomach and imagine the colors of the mandala sliding out of it and flooding your heart.

With each deep breath, the colors spread out from your heart to the rest of your body.

With your entire body overflowing with colors, imagine yourself surrounded by a pink cloud.

Be aware that pink is the color that activates love, emotion, and understanding; it softens you and opens you to each other.

In your thoughts, send your energies flowing around you, from left to right, until you feel you are in the middle of the pink flow.

Hold this thought for at least ten breaths.

Think of your wedding and connect with the joy and excitement that you felt then.

Close your eyes and commit yourself to change something small within you that upsets your partner, in order for your relationship to be perfect.

Take five deep breaths and open your eyes.

Wedding Day: Meditation for the Bride and Groom

First of all—congratulations! Your wedding day is the one that determines the energy for your married lives, so the happy couple should strive to be as relaxed as possible, in spite of all the pressure.

Practice the meditation together, either lying down or standing up and holding hands.

Suitable healing crystals: Rose Quartz, Moonstone

Meditation

Gaze at the colors of the mandala and inhale them into your stomach while taking ten deep and relaxed breaths.

Imagine yourself under the wedding canopy or standing at the altar and the heavens welcoming with love the special bond that has been created between you.

Hope in your heart that this bond will continue for the rest of your lives.

Send an energetic ray of love from your heart to your future wife/husband.

Welcome the ray with joy and send back a ray of your own.

Each time you look at your wedding ring, you are reminded that your souls have become one soul, and that its round shape represents perfection and circularity.

Take a vow in your heart to do everything in your power to maintain the perfection of your marriage.

Take ten deep breaths and relax.

Enhancing Intimacy

After reading the section in the first chapter, Getting Started, that explains spirituality, you surely understand that spirituality plays an important role in intimacy issues. Change does not happen of its own accord, so you should prepare a list of things that you would like to change in your relationship. Continue to practice this meditation until you feel a positive change in your life. Together with your imagination, the meditation creates a positive and pleasant atmosphere for change in your relationship. For example: If your partner doesn't listen to you, start listening to him/her yourself and he/she will begin to reveal (on his or her own) a willingness to do the same. If you feel that your partner should make an urgent change, take a good look at yourself—maybe it's you who needs to undergo an urgent change. The equation is: If you change, he/she will change. Try it and see. Each time things improve; work on another issue on your list.

Suitable healing crystals: Rose Quartz, Moonstone

Meditation

Begin with the breathing exercises at the beginning of the part "Meditations for the Soul."

Gaze at the center of this mandala for at least two minutes.

Introduce the color pink into your heart and soul by taking deep breaths for at least one minute.

In your imagination, surround your partner with the color pink.

Watch as the pink is absorbed and softens him/her.

Now he/she can become completely attentive to you and you can say anything you want.

Send your partner love and, in your mind, send him/her a desire to change.

Imagine an arc of light passing from your heart to his/her heart.

Hold this thought for two minutes.

Close your eyes and imagine this change taking place.

Observe the two of you able to talk freely about everything.

Imagine the love renewing itself in your lives and feel happy and full of joy.

Count to three silently and open your eyes.

Love and Unity Within the Family

As the mother of the family, you have the power to bring about positive change, such as unity and love; I therefore recommend practicing this meditation frequently.

Suitable healing crystals: Rose Quartz, Moonstone, Malachite

Meditation

Practice the breathing exercise at the beginning of the part "Meditations for the Soul."

Gaze at the center of this mandala for at least two minutes.

Take deep breaths into your heart for a full minute.

Imagine your entire family sitting around you.

Imagine a colorful arc of love passing from your heart into the hearts of each and every one of your relatives (in your imagination, you appear as a fountain).

Hold this thought for at least two minutes.

Feel an improvement in your existing relationship and sense genuine mutual concern within your family.

Close your eyes for a moment and create arcs of love among all of you.

In your heart, pray for everyone to receive what he/she really needs right now and pass it on to him/her via the arc of colors.

Collect the arcs of love and colors back into your heart.

Count silently to three and open your eyes.

When a Relationship Comes to an End

In order to move on with your life after a breakup, prepare a list of negative things that you remember from the partner from whom you are separated and take a good look at it. Do you really want to live with all this? Don't say "yes," just because you are afraid to be alone; strive for something better for yourself. After this meditation, when you feel ready for love, practice the meditation for finding your soul mate.

Suitable healing crystals: Rose Quartz, Moonstone, Chrysocolla, Amazonite

Meditation

Begin with the breathing exercise at the beginning of the part "Meditations for the Soul."

Gaze at the center of this mandala for at least two minutes.

Introduce the color pink into your heart as you take deep breaths for at least one minute.

Look into your heart and, with each breath you take, use the color pink to heal your heart.

Imagine yourself gluing together any breaks and cracks that you find.

As you meditate, exhale from all your cells all the energies left behind by your former partner.

Breathe deeply and hold this thought for at least three minutes.

Close your eyes and disperse the pink color to all parts of your body during the next ten breaths.

Count silently to three and open your eyes.

Relationships at Work

You likely spend a large part of your day at work, so it is extremely important for you to enjoy being there. If something has happened and the place is no longer pleasant, you should take action to improve matters. You have the ability to change things even if you are convinced that others, who are not attentive to you or who are not interested in being in your company, are to blame. It is the energy that you transmit from within yourself that will determine the quality of your relationships and, of course, positive energies (love, patience, joy, and calm) will draw positive reactions from your peers. Try it and see.

At work, try to avoid discussing your personal problems with your colleagues; this draws negative energies and can snowball into a situation that cannot be remedied. If you feel the need to get things off your chest, write it all down on a piece of paper, which you can then destroy.

Suitable healing crystals: Rose Quartz, Chrysanthemum Crystal, Rhodonite, Turritella Agate

Meditation

Gaze at the center of this mandala for at least two minutes.

Practice the breathing exercise at the beginning of the part "Meditations for the Soul."

Imagine the person to whom you wish to send positive energies.

See how light and colors fill his/her heart and, from there, spreads throughout his/her body.

Wish him/her love, joy, and fulfillment so that he/she can become relaxed, encouraging, supportive, patient, generous, and considerate in his/her job.

Gaze at the mandala and hold this thought as you breathe deeply for at least two minutes. Close your eyes and see how his/her attitude to you changes and how your life changes as a result.

Silently count backward from ten to one and open your eyes.

Good luck!

Recharging Your Energy

Meditation

Sit in a straight-backed chair (rather than a soft lounger).

Feel your feet on the floor. Feel the connection with the earth.

Imagine a bright white ball of light over your head.

Allow the ball to descend toward your head and to fill your skull halfway (down to your eyes).

Feel the energy generated by the intense light filling your body,

flowing down your spine,

the length of your legs,

and down to your feet.

Draw exactly the amount of energy you need from the ball.

If you feel any pressure in your head, you can create a kind of "extension cord" to the ground from your heels to balance your energy consumption.

Close your eyes, and hold this charging position for about four or five minutes.

Now release the ball of light back into infinity.

Feel your feet and your connection to the ground.

Open your eyes.

Confidence and Self-Esteem

Suitable healing crystals: I recommend drinking water that has been infused with a Tiger's Eye healing crystal. Lay the crystal on your navel as you meditate.

Meditation

Gaze at the colors of this mandala for at least three minutes while taking deep breaths into your stomach.

Begin with the breathing exercise at the beginning of the part "Meditations for the Soul."

Imagine a spiral of yellow/gold light hovering above you.

Exhale all your failures, disappointments, and shortcomings into the middle of the spiral and watch it thicken each time you exhale.

Now, with one breath, sever the ring and release it back into infinity.

Now imagine another, new spiral, in a yellow/gold color, this time connected by a cord to your navel.

Fill the ring with positive thoughts of success and achievement. As the ring grows, draw it inwards, into your stomach, and allow the feeling of confidence to spread throughout your body.

Create a new reality for yourself and view this reality as if it was a movie being shown on a screen.

Close your eyes, smile, enjoy the new movie, and know that everything is possible.

Count silently to seven and open your eyes.

Feel that you have pulled this strength into your life.

Enthusiasm

You feel a lack of enthusiasm when you can't value the things you have—otherwise, you would wake up each morning full of enthusiasm, with the knowledge that everything has its cause and its unseen order. You would take advantage of every minute of the day in every sphere of your life, including your neighbors, your in-laws, your wife/husband, children, the rising sun, the amazing landscape, the tree that has just budded, the parking space that is waiting just for you, etc. You should start paying attention and value what you have, because nothing can be taken for granted.

Suitable healing crystals: Rhodochrosite, Rhodonite, Dendritic Agate, Carnelian

Meditation

Begin with the breathing exercise at the beginning of the part "Meditations for the Soul."

Gaze at the colors of this mandala for at least three minutes.

See yourself enthusing over everything, as you did in the past, in your youth, in your childhood.

Be glad, since awakening every morning anew is a thing that should not be taken for granted, and appreciate every minute of your day.

Inhale this thought with ten inhalations of the color orange.

Close your eyes for a moment and think of the color blue.

Silently count to ten and open your eyes.

Creativity

If you find it hard to create, to amaze people with a new idea, or to realize a childhood dream in which you turn into a "star," practice this meditation before you go to sleep and a few times during the day. Good luck.

Suitable healing crystals: Red Jasper, Citrine, Sandstone, Smoky Quartz, Sapphire

Meditation

Breathe deeply into your stomach and gaze at the center of the mandala for one minute.

Take five more deep breaths and think about your coccyx (the lowest bone in your back).

Now gaze at the colors, and enjoy the creativity expressed in the mandala for at least one minute.

Connect to the amazing ability and creativity of the artist.

Focus on the subject you need assistance with.

Wish for the ability to realize your idea, whether it be to draw, to write, to compose, etc.

Close your eyes and imagine your creation coming into being.

Gaze once again at the mandala and breathe the colors into your throat five more times.

Count backward silently from ten to one and complete the meditation.

Saying You Are Sorry

By apologizing, you recognize the fact that you are not perfect. Often your ego prevents you from behaving with human dignity. This type of ego holds you back. On the positive side, the ego provides you with a jumping board to push yourself forward, to reinforce your desires and aspirations; but not at the expense of others.

Quite possibly, the apology you owe could be for something you said yesterday, or even for things that were said years ago. It's high time to take a step forward. By practicing this meditation, you will prepare yourself for saying you are sorry in real time.

Suitable healing crystals: Chrysoprase, Apache Tear

Meditation

Gaze at the center of this mandala for at least three minutes.

Begin with the breathing exercise at the beginning of the part "Meditations for the Soul."

Imagine yourself sitting in an armchair and facing you is someone to whom you owe an apology.

Listen to his/her side of the story.

Allow him/her to explain everything and you **just listen**.

Understand him, even if you find it really difficult.

As you meditate, apologize to him with all your heart (and subsequently practice doing so out loud when you are alone in the room).

Watch as he/she stands up and comes over to embrace you and accept your apology.

Feel the relief in your heart and in your soul.

Close your eyes and wish that you could have the ability to apologize as well in reality, in the near future.

Count to five and open your eyes.

Joy and Happiness

Depression and sadness accumulate in your spleen. Depression and sadness are types of negative energy and, in order to be healthy and happy, you must know how to shake them off. Practicing meditation on a regular basis will help you achieve change in your awareness. Research shows that happy people are healthier and have longer life expectancies; why shouldn't you be like that, too?

Take a look at the section on "Joy, Laughter, and Music" in the first chapter, Getting Started, and, several times a day, scan the table of the 72 Names of God.

Suitable healing crystals: I suggest you drink water infused with Carnelian and, while you meditate, you can hold a Snowflake Obsidian in your hand.

Meditation

Gaze at this mandala and breathe deeply for at least one minute.

Try to recall a moment of happiness and focus on it.

As you gaze at the colors, inhale that moment until you feel relief.

Now breathe the shades of orange—the color of happiness—deep into your lower abdomen.

Ask for the strength to get through this period happily.

Lay your hands on your abdomen and feel warmth spreading through your hands.

Hold this position until you feel better and then release your hands.

Discarding Anger

Meditation

Breathe deep into your stomach and gaze at the colors of the mandala for at least two minutes.

Practice two consecutive rounds of the breathing exercise at the beginning of the part "Meditations for the Soul."

Recite to yourself out loud the following declarations:

"Anger accumulates in my liver and causes energy blockages that disturb the perfect function of my body."

"When I am angry, my body doesn't manage to clean away the toxins and medications."

"Anger causes me to feel tired and worn out, because it is a negative energy."

"From now on, I choose to connect to the energies of health and happiness."

Inhale the colors deeply into the area of your liver (located in the abdomen, beneath the last right-hand rib) and breathe out the anger.

Continue breathing in this way for two to three minutes.

Imagine that each breath enters the liver and calms the source of the anger.

Close your eyes and think of the color blue.

Silently ask to be able to control your reactions and to lower your anger level until you no longer feel anger.

Keep breathing this thought for at least three minutes.

Count silently to four and open your eyes.

Abundance

This meditation helps you realize your desires by influencing the energies around you and create a new reality for yourself by attracting into your life those energies that symbolize abundance. I recommend practicing this meditation immediately before falling asleep. Prepare a list of the material things that you think are necessary (work, money, a home, a car, etc.) and recite it each time you practice this meditation (you could leave the list with this book).

Suitable healing crystals: Citrine, Turritella Agate

Meditation

Begin with the breathing exercise at the beginning of the part "Meditations for the Soul."

Gaze at the center of this mandala for at least two minutes and draw energy from it into your upper abdomen toward the solar plexus chakra, the energy center of desire and ambition.

Go through your list and imagine yourself residing in the house of your dreams, driving the car you have always wanted, working at a job that you love and that suits your talents.

Live these moments as if they are real, behave as if you already have it all and feel relaxed.

Hold this "have it all" thought for as long as you need to and, with each breath, free yourself of your feeling of poverty.

Declare to the Universe that you value everything you have as you wish for things that can make your life more comfortable.

Gaze at the mandala for as long as you want, while drawing the colors into your upper abdomen.

When you sever yourself from it, close your eyes. Count to ten and open them slowly.

Accustom yourself to your surroundings.

Feel that you have awakened a "have it all" reality in the Universe.

Protection

This is best practiced before sleep and after all other meditations.

Suitable healing crystals: Tourmaline, Turquoise, Malachite, Jet, Cat's Eye

Meditation

Gaze at this mandala for at least one minute, while breathing deeply.

Imagine a web of golden threads surrounding your aura.

The web protects you and is there even if you don't really see it.

The web sees to it that your accumulated energy will be maintained.

The web is with you, protecting you throughout the day and night.

Count silently to four and open your eyes.

Trauma

I recommend a full daily immersion in water, preferably in any kind of natural water source, but, if there is no choice, in an outdoor pool. Before immersion, ask for the water to purify your traumatic energies from within and without. Study the section "Ritual Immersion: Spiritual and Energetic Purification" in the first chapter, Getting Started.

Suitable healing crystals: Rose Quartz, Amethyst

Meditation

Begin with the breathing exercise at the beginning of the part "Meditations for the Soul."

Gaze at the colors of this mandala and breathe deeply for four minutes.

Now imagine yourself floating inside your body, and check where your energy has been damaged as a result of the trauma you have experienced.

Place your hands over every area you feel you need to mend and stay there for a while.

Repair it with the help of the colors of the mandala and your thoughts.

Breathe into the area without removing your hands, until you have refilled it with energy.

Continue to another area of your body.

When you have completed healing your body, close your eyes and imagine yourself surrounded by the color purple.

Count silently to ten and open your eyes.

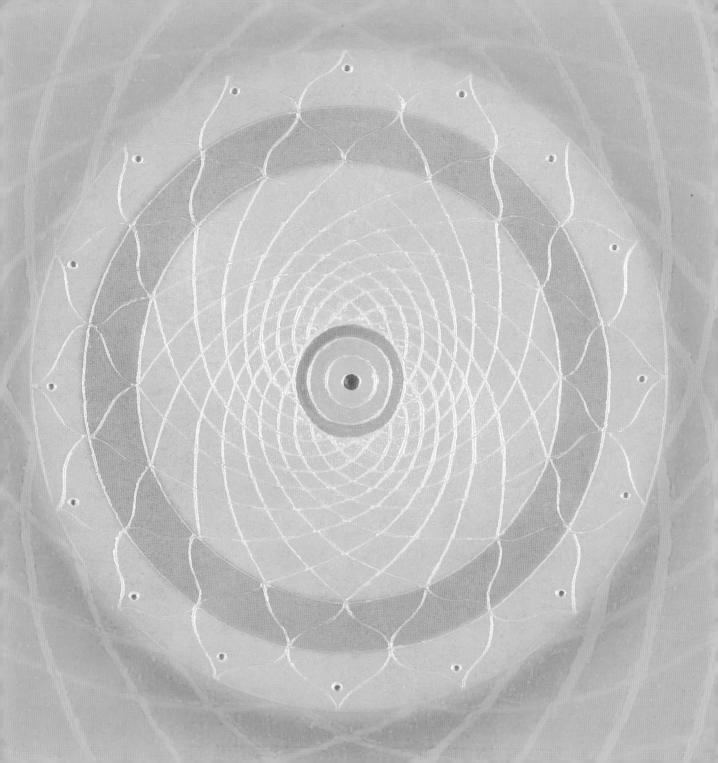

Fears and Anxieties

Fear presents a problem that is not easy to solve because it is relative and personal and takes a different form in each person who suffers from it. It is easier to fight fear if you are aware that fear is an illusion. You can start understanding this by looking at different kinds of fear; for example, not everyone is afraid of dogs, flying, the dark, or of being alone. It is understandable in the case of everyone being afraid of the same threat, for example, war. Yet everyone has a personal fear that prevents him/her from moving on in life. If you fight your fear, you'll conquer it and enable yourself to burst through the walls that are enclosing you. What do you have to lose? I recommend practicing the meditations Balance of the Body and Soul and Cleaning the Aura in this book. Practice this meditation while lying down on your back.

Suitable healing crystals (to be placed in the area of your knees as you meditate): Obsidian, Hematite, Black Tourmaline. Hold in your hand: Snowflake Obsidian or Turquoise.

Meditation

Begin with the breathing exercise at the beginning of the part "Meditations for the Soul."

Take deep breaths into your stomach and imagine your breath flowing down to your legs.

Now open imaginary orifices—one in the lower back and one beneath each knee.

Breathe deeply and, as you exhale, expel all your fears out through these imaginary orifices, down to the ground.

Continue breathing with this thought in mind until you feel more relaxed.

Gaze at the colors of this mandala and inhale the color turquoise as you take ten deep breaths.

Close your eyes and imagine yourself closing the orifices.

Think of yourself being surrounded by positive energies and light.

Inhale the light until your body is illuminated from head to toe.

Take ten deep breaths into your abdomen and open your eyes.

Identifying Your Fears

Fears are sometimes impressions that you drag with you from unpleasant experiences in your past, or from previous incarnations (these will be fears that have no explanation yet they are with you all your life). For example, if you have experienced unrequited love, you will find it hard to open up to someone new because you will fear feeling the same pain, or if you failed in some task or other, you won't retry it for fear of failing again.

However, if you watch a toddler taking his first steps, you see that he falls time after time, but continues to try and never gives up. You too, were once a baby, and you, too, have the ability to persevere and not to be afraid of trying again.

Fear is an illusion that prevents you from moving forward. By identifying, recognizing, and labeling your fears, you can restrict their development, as if you are confining them in a small box. This is the beginning of the process by which you can come to terms with your fears.

Suitable healing crystals: Tourmaline, Tiger's Eye, Onyx, Sodalite, Jet, Amethyst, Calcite

Meditation

Take deep breaths into your abdomen while gazing at the mandala for two minutes.

Imagine you can look into yourself and identify your fear. Imagine your fear as a stain that you can wrap in white light. Let white light flow toward your fear until it is completely illuminated.

Identify your fear and label it. For example: Fear of financial loss, fear of heights, separation anxiety, etc. Look straight into your fear as you gaze at the mandala for two minutes.

Close your eyes and think about courage and resourcefulness. Ask in your heart to have more of these traits within you.

Count to ten and open your eyes.

Note: Study this book and choose more meditations that will help you change a situation that causes you to feel fear. Practice the Antidote meditation. For example: for treating a fear of financial loss, choose the Abundance meditation; for claustrophobia, choose the Claustrophobia and Fear of Flying meditation.

Attention Deficit Disorder (ADD & ADHD)

I recommend learning more about the mandala in the first chapter, Getting Started. By focusing on the center of the mandala for a number of minutes, you can improve, in time, your powers of concentration, your thought processes, your organizational skills, and your memory. Painting the blank mandalas provided with this book is another helpful practice.

Suitable healing crystal: Amethyst

Meditation for Adults

Gaze at the center of this mandala for five minutes.

As you take deep breaths into your abdomen, draw the colors through your forehead and into your head.

Imagine the right and left sides of your brain being painted the colors of the mandala.

Breathe in deeply and wish yourself to become as well organized, accurate, and focused as the symmetrical shapes of the mandala.

Focus on your inner self and ask for your memory to be infinite.

Close your eyes for a moment and continue seeing the mandala and its colors in your mind's eye.

Take five deep breaths and open your eyes.

Meditation for Children

Show the child the mandala and ask him/her to gaze into its center.

Don't force him/her to sit for longer than he/she can.

You can also place the mandala on the desk where the child does his/her homework, so that the mandala will be constantly visible and the child can gaze at it frequently.

Explain to the child the importance of frequently gazing at the mandala. Refer back to the details of the adult meditation and in the mandala section of the first chapter, Getting Started.

If the child is sufficiently mature, he/she can be taught how to breathe deeply while gazing at the mandala.

Claustrophobia and Fear of Flying

There is more to lose than to gain when life is governed by fear. How much time do you spend on alternative routes instead of flying or taking an elevator? This meditation will help you control your fear and enable you to be free.

If you encounter difficulty practicing this meditation and/or experience harsh feelings as a result of it, just practice as long as you can every day (but at least half a minute).

Practice this meditation until you feel ready to attempt the real thing. Practice may continue for six months or longer, but only if you persevere will you succeed.

Suitable healing crystals: Tourmaline, Tiger's Eye, Onyx, Sodalite, Jet, Amethyst, Calcite

Meditation

Gaze at this mandala for at least a minute.

Repeat the breathing exercise at the beginning of the part "Meditations for the Soul" twice.

Imagine yourself in a place where you want to feel comfortable (a plane, elevator, walk-in-closet, a crowded hall, etc.) and sharply exhale the feeling of pressure as you gaze at the colors of the mandala.

Allow yourself to be flooded with the feeling of fear. Perspire and shudder if necessary; at the same time, breathe deeply and exhale the fear.

You'll be looking fear in the eyes.

Slowly close your eyes and imagine that you are able to confront your fear. See yourself carrying out everything that you find difficult and enjoying every minute.

Keep breathing with this thought in mind for as long as you like and then open your eyes.

Successful Negotiation

This meditation should be practiced before a meeting. The meditation will help only if your intentions are honorable. Remember that we are not able to see the whole picture and that there is always a chance of something good happening even if it doesn't appear so at the moment.

I recommend wearing a shirt in any shade of yellow or mustard. If you have a problem with this color, practice by wearing a yellow or mustard-colored T-shirt at home until you become accustomed to it.

Suitable healing crystals: Citrine, Turritella Agate, Jet

Meditation

Gaze at the center of the mandala for at least two minutes and inhale the color yellow into your upper abdomen.

Now practice the breathing exercise at the beginning of the part "Meditations for the Soul."

Imagine the person you are about to meet sitting in his/her office, or yours.

Send him/her the color yellow that you hold within you, from your upper abdomen to his/her upper abdomen.

Watch as the color is absorbed into his/her abdomen and flows throughout his/her body.

Transfer by thought your proposal to him/her, down to the last detail and show him/her how great it is.

Close your eyes and imagine him/her accepting the proposal and loving your idea.

See in your imagination that the deal is struck, and the papers are signed.

Breathe deeply into your abdomen and open your eyes.

Passing an Exam

Exams and tests are not only something you pass at school. Everyday activity provides you with many small, apparently insignificant tests. If you get through them easily, you'll be given strength for the real tests that life has in store for you. You should see these small tests as a springboard for a better reality and be able to turn every hardship into a blessing.

Suitable healing crystals: Amethyst, Citrine, Quartz, Blue Calcite

Meditation

Gaze at the yellow center of the mandala for a minute and think about your stomach.

The color yellow arouses your desire to succeed. Breathe with this thought in mind for an additional minute.

Now gaze for a minute at the purple part of the mandala and think about your head. The color purple awakens the gray cells of your brain, reinforces your memory, and allows you to be more focused.

All the information you need to remember for this exam is now being shown on a big screen and you can look at it at all times.

Now gaze for another minute at the center of the mandala and allow all the colors to influence you simultaneously.

Close your eyes and imagine that you are succeeding and achieving high grades.

Count to ten and open your eyes.

Good luck!

Treating Addictions: Smoking, Eating, Alcohol, and Drugs

Addiction gives the soul a feeling of fulfillment and satisfaction, but everyone knows that this is merely an illusion. If you wish to be clean of addiction, you must find the right things to fill your life and cause you to feel truly rewarded. Positive substitutes for addiction can take the form of sport, creativity, volunteering, or helping society.

It is also a good idea to study spiritual subjects such as healing or Kabbalah, which in time will help you look deep inside yourself. Spiritual study, whatever the subject, fills your soul, leads you to accept reality with love, helps you to cope with hardship, and erases the feeling of emptiness that leads to the onset of addiction.

This meditation should be practiced regularly, twice a day.

Suitable healing crystal: Amethyst

Meditation

Gaze at the center of this mandala for at least two minutes. With each breath you take, internalize your determination to be clean.

Continue gazing at the mandala for another minute as you reinforce your willpower in your mind.

Send the colors flowing into the damaged organ (with smoking, it's the lungs; removing a food addiction involves the digestive system; with alcohol and drug addition, it's the liver).

Imagine the colors being absorbed and healing the damaged tissues.

Now disperse the yellow color in the mandala throughout your upper abdomen, into the energy center that is located there and is responsible for your willpower.

Fill it with the strength to fulfill your decision.

Close your eyes and imagine yourself healthy and happy.

Remain like this for at least one minute.

Count to five and open your eyes.

Female Fertility

This meditation is good for women who have no physical problem, but have been unable to become pregnant. Tension, stress, and an overactive thought process are all possible obstacles to becoming pregnant, so general relaxation therapies, such as massage, shiatsu, reflexology, and meditation can all help. They cause the body to open up and to heal, and the resulting emotional tranquility makes it possible for a pregnancy to take place. This meditation should be repeated at least once a day. Many women have received this meditation from me in the form of a work page and became pregnant immediately, after many years of waiting. If you are undergoing a course of in vitro fertilization (IVF), this meditation can complement and speed up the process. I highly recommend following the advice in the chapter on spiritual immersion and purification in the first chapter, Getting Started. Good luck to you, dear women!!

Suitable healing crystal: Drink water infused with a Ruby healing crystal. You can also lay this crystal on your navel as you meditate. You must stop using the crystal as soon as you become pregnant.

Meditation

Gaze at the mandala on the opposite page for at least three minutes.

Practice the breathing exercise at the beginning of the part "Meditations for the Soul."

Imagine your lower abdomen as a vessel that fills with the color orange with every breath you take.

Color with orange the inside of your womb, your ovaries, and fallopian tubes and imagine the color being absorbed into them.

Color your entire uterus with orange and continue breathing for at least two minutes more, while gazing at the mandala.

Imagine yourself pregnant and experiencing all the stages of your pregnancy.

Now close your eyes, feel your belly growing to the size of a nine-month pregnancy and imagine yourself giving birth.

When you have finished, count to four silently and open your eyes.

Tip: Use the pressure point described in the PMS meditation and repeat it several times a day.

Stuttering and Speech Impediments

A fellow student of mine suffered from a stutter on certain letters of the alphabet. After using this meditation in class, he was able to talk freely, without a trace of a stutter. The sound of the word Om creates a vibration of positive energy that surrounds you and releases blocked energies in your throat and vocal cords (yes, you will sound like a Buddhist monk).

This meditation should be practiced at least twice every day.

Suitable healing crystals: Blue Lace Agate, Lapis, Kunzite

Meditation

Practice the breathing exercise at the beginning of the part "Meditations for the Soul."

Gaze at the center of this mandala for three minutes and imagine the colors flowing into your throat.

Sit upright and focus on the letters OM ॐ.

Take a deep breath and chant the mantra OM; make it as drawn out as possible.

Keep repeating the mantra for at least three consecutive minutes.

Close your eyes, feel yourself surrounded by vibrations of positive energy, and imagine yourself holding a conversation, your speech fluent and relaxed.

Count to ten and open your eyes.

Meditation for World Peace

Positive thoughts, dispatched by large numbers of people, can bring about miracles.

You, too, can help with the power of your thoughts. Send positive thoughts of peace for your country and for the whole world and this thought can attract a different energy to any region you choose. The energy of peace and quiet will slowly change the current situation into one that is positive and stress-free.

Meditation is one way of changing the world and making it a better place to live in.

Meditation

Gaze at the center of the mandala, taking deep breaths for at least a minute. Allow the colors to integrate into your awareness.

Now gaze at a part of the mandala that has the color pink. (Pink is the color of cosmic love.)

Imagine you are sending a message of love to all the people in the country and to all the people in the world.

Imagine that peace reigns throughout the world.

Gaze at the circle of people holding hands in the mandala, and broadcast a message of unity that includes all the people in the country and all over the globe.

Close your eyes for a moment and imagine the world as a more balanced place and the people in it living in harmony.

Take five deep breaths and open your eyes to a wonderful world.

Your Birthday: The Most Special Day of the Year

Your birthday is the day on which you can connect to your inherent potential and to "go back in time" to the moment of your birth—a time when the program of your life, of the person you were meant to be, was perfect. Each of us arrives in this world with a kind of preordained program and it is our job to implement it in the best way possible.

Of course, there are obstacles and glitches on the way that draw our attention away from whatever really needs to happen. This original birthday program contains all the tools we need for realizing our potential and succeeding in life. You should connect to this day's energy, because without it, it will be difficult to fulfill your dreams.

Each year on this day, return and connect to the source of your energy and think of the things you aspire to draw into your life with greater strength. I suggest you prepare and memorize a list of all the concrete and spiritual things (the physical and mental things) that you wish for yourself and that you would like to happen to you during the coming year (until your next birthday). The introduction to the various zodiac signs might give the impression that emphasis was laid mainly on the negative aspects of each sign, but bear in mind that the objective here is to achieve change. In order to extract the most out of it, you should read, decide that you don't wish to be associated with these traits, and make the appropriate changes. There is no point in reinforcing positive traits that you know are yours anyway. If one or more characteristics in the meditation does not apply to you, erase it, replace it with a different personality trait you do have, and that you want to improve and change. If you fail to connect at all to any of the personality traits in the meditation, you can always write to me at *argaman@netvision.net.il* and I will be happy to help.

Most important of all, on your birthday, you become a channel of positive energy and you should embrace everyone, so you can share with others the enormous amounts of energy with which you have been endowed during that day. It will do them good.

Note: This meditation should be practiced several times on your birthday, because it is then that the available energy is strongest.

Aries—March 21 to April 20

First, reread the introduction to this section: Your Birthday: The Most Special Day of the Year.

Aries is the first sign of the Zodiac, so if you were born under it you will feel very important, because this is the energy with which you came to this world. You will, therefore, find it hard to listen to others, to see their needs and to understand them (although you may appear attentive and focused). People born under the sign of Aries have the ability to leap energetically into new things, but find it hard to persevere and complete them, because you lose interest and are easily bored and want to experience the energy of new things. You'll always be at the center of things, in the front line. You are influenced by Mars and, because of this, you are high-strung, quick to respond, and have a short temper.

Meditation

Gaze at the mandala as you take ten deep breaths into your abdomen.

Imagine the skies opening and special energy flowing down to you, an energy that will allow you to identify your priorities, to give in when necessary, to really listen to those around you, to use your natural energy, and to push forward with ideas. This energy will give you the strength to persevere in what you are doing and finish what you've started. This energy will also help you think of others and remind you that when you share, you receive more, and will provide you with the ability to control your anger and your reactions.

(Change, erase, or pencil in those traits that you would like to change in yourself.)

This energy flows like a waterfall over your head.

Open an imaginary opening at the top of your head (the crown chakra), through which you allow this energy to move through your entire body.

Close your eyes and think of all the things you want to achieve as you gaze at the mandala for five minutes.

Imagine your life changing accordingly.

Think of today's special energy flowing toward everyone who is important to you.

Count another five deep breaths of the colors of the mandala and open your eyes.

Taurus—April 21 to May 20

First, reread the introduction to this section: Your Birthday: The Most Special Day of the Year.

People born under this sign are known for their stubbornness, so their neck is the stiffest and most painful parts of their bodies. They have a wonderful ability to always see the cup as half full. Ostensibly, this is a positive trait, but you are so obsessed with the good side of things that it sometimes takes you a few years to understand that you are in a situation that requires drastic change, whether at work or in relationships. By nature, you will choose not to exert yourself and not to move too much, just like a bull. Taurus is influenced by the planet Venus, which affects beauty and aestheticism in the world; you will no doubt choose, therefore, to surround yourself with good-looking people. By doing so, however, you will miss out on the possibility of seeing other people's inner beauty, which often is much more intense.

Meditation

Gaze at the mandala and take ten deep breaths into your abdomen.

Imagine the skies opening and special energy flowing down to you.

This energy will enable you to get out of your comfort zone and start doing things, and will help you relinquish your stubbornness and flow along with life. The energy will help you see what you need to change in yourself, even though everything seems perfect to you. That energy will enable you to see the soul in everyone you meet (beauty is more than skin deep . . .). That energy will enable you to listen to spiritual messages, even if they are not logical.

(Change, erase, or pencil in those traits that you would like to change in yourself.)

This energy flows like a waterfall over your head. Open an imaginary opening in the top of your head (crown chakra), through which you will allow the energy to flow into your body. Think of all the things you would like to achieve and gaze at the center of the mandala as you breathe five times. Close your eyes and imagine your life changing accordingly. Think of yourself sharing today's special energy with everyone who is important to you. Count five deep breaths and open your eyes.

Gemini—May 21 to June 21

First, reread the introduction to this section: Your Birthday: The Most Special Day of the Year.

People born under Gemini are highly intelligent, quickly bored by new things, especially things that are obvious and familiar (you are capable of beginning a four-year course of study and dropping out after three, without batting an eye). You are influenced by the planet Jupiter, which affects nimbleness of mind and action, which makes you good in communications and marketing, although you are also impatient toward those who are slower than you. You are capable of loving deeply and profoundly, more than one man or more than one woman, and you are convinced that this is all right. Also, you tend to completely change your mind with every new piece of information you acquire. You find it hard to be constant and to take responsibility. Part of the problem lies in the fact that in your soul, there still lurks the child you once were, so that there is a naughtiness about you, a love for and an understanding of children, and you always look better than your real age.

Meditation

Gaze at the mandala on the opposite page and take ten deep breaths into your abdomen.

Imagine the skies opening up and a special energy flowing down to you, an energy that allows you to complete what you have begun, the energy to be inquisitive to know what the next sentence will be that you will hear, the energy to sit still for a moment of quiet and to be patient toward those around you, to be mature when necessary and to take responsibility for your actions.

(Change, erase, or pencil in those traits that you would like to change in yourself).

The energy flows like a waterfall over your head.

In the middle of your head (the crown chakra), an imaginary orifice opens, through which the energy flows into your body. Think of all the things you want to achieve and gaze at the mandala as you count five breaths.

Close your eyes for a moment and imagine your life changing accordingly.

In your mind, let today's special energy flow to everyone who is important to you.

Count another five deep breaths, inhaling and exhaling the color red, and open your eyes.

The Art of Mandala Meditation

Cancer—June 22 to July 22

First, reread the introduction to this section: Your Birthday: The Most Special Day of the Year.

As someone born under the sign of Cancer, you are influenced by the Moon, which makes you more susceptible to feelings than to simple, logical thought. When you love, your love knows no bounds and you can sometimes suffocate your partner. It is hard for you to shake off the past and to move on, with confidence, into the future. Every decision is accompanied by serious uncertainty and even after the decision is made, you always take a step back or move like a crab on the beach, walking along sideways. If you are lucky, you make some progress. Since you are influenced by emotions, your moods tend to be up and down, especially down. I suggest you choose a profession such as teaching, medicine, or something in which your naturally giving nature finds expression. Also, a connection to the energy of water is essential for emotional stability, and I warmly recommend that you read the section "Ritual Immersion" in the first chapter, Getting Started.

Meditation

Take ten deep breaths into your abdomen as you gaze at the mandala.

Imagine the skies opening and a special energy flowing down to you, an energy that allows you to let go of the past. It is an energy of independence and absolute certainty that allows you to decide easily, to accept responsibility and to stick to it, to be sensitive to others and to allow them their own breathing space and independence, and to always be connected to energies of joy.

(Change, erase, or pencil in those traits that you would like to change in yourself.)

This energy flows like a waterfall over your head. At the top of your head (crown chakra) an imaginary orifice is opened, through which the energy will flow through your body. Think of all the things you'd like to achieve and gaze at the mandala while taking five breaths. Close your eyes for a moment and imagine your life changing accordingly.

In your mind, let today's special energy flow to everyone who is important to you.

Count another five deep breaths with the color red and open your eyes.

Leo—July 23 to August 22

First, reread the introduction to this section: Your Birthday: The Most Special Day of the Year.

People born under the sign of Leo are influenced by the Sun. The sun's rays can reach easily and pour warmth, light, and life into everything, just as you can. You are the kind of person who cannot be ignored, just as it is impossible to ignore the sun. That quality makes you believe you are the most important of all and mustn't be ignored. You'll always turn up first for everything and catch the best seat; unless you arrive last with a flurry of noise and feathers—and everyone else will have to notice you. It is not easy to argue with someone as strong as the sun, and you should understand that it is hard being in your vicinity all day long, feeling the scalding energy of the sun. As you work on changing your character traits, you should focus on your overactive ego and try to reduce it. Try to focus on your surrounds and your peers, and make positive use of the influential power you received as a gift. If you don't find this to be an accurate description of your character, you might consider showing this page to someone close to you who has known you a number of years, and ask for an opinion. In most cases, you'll get a confirmation.

Meditation

Take ten deep breaths into your abdomen and gaze at the mandala.

Imagine the skies opening and a special energy flowing down to you, an energy that will allow you to sense other people. It is an energy that will help you work on your ego; let others have a say, too; warm things without burning them; and to illuminate without burning fuses. In other words, to give life.

(Change, erase, or pencil in those traits that you would like to change in yourself.)

This energy flows like a waterfall over your head. At the top of your head (crown chakra) an imaginary orifice is opened, through which the energy will flow through your body. Think of all the things you'd like to achieve and gaze at the mandala and take five breaths.

Close your eyes for a moment and imagine your life changing accordingly.

In your mind, let today's special energy flow to everyone who is important to you.

Count another five deep breaths and open your eyes.

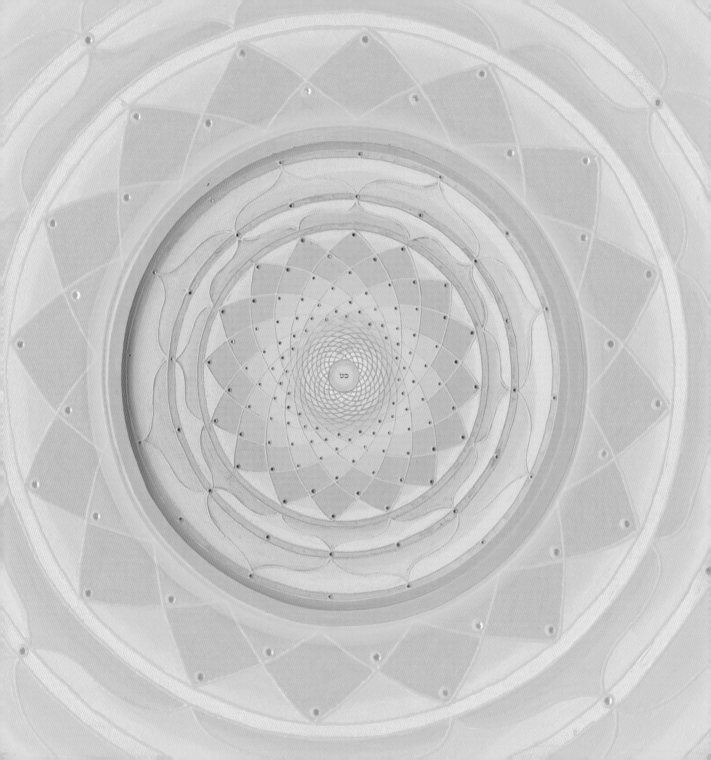

Virgo—August 23 to September 22

First, reread the introduction to this section: Your Birthday: The Most Special Day of the Year.

People born under the sign of Virgo are notoriously critical and aspire to perfection. You are capable of seeing every single fault in your peers, but can't understand that these faults are identifiable only because they exist in you too. In other words, everything you see in another person exists in you as well. The ability to see the big picture has been taken from you and given to people born under the sign Gemini, who share the planet Jupiter with you. You were left with the ability to see the details. You must accept that not everything is as perfect and organized as you would like or think it should be. Some people find their own order in their untidiness and there is nothing wrong with that. You were born in a month during which the world undergoes inner cleansing and spiritual purification, which is why you have a strong intuition that has to be tidy and squeaky-clean. Cleanliness is something internal, belonging to the soul, and it is there where you should work on it. I warmly recommend reading the section that deals with spirituality in the first chapter, Getting Started.

Meditation

Gaze at the mandala on the opposite page and breathe deeply into your abdomen ten times. Imagine the skies opening and a special energy flowing down over you—an energy that will allow you to accept others as they are, will help you criticize no one but yourself. It is an energy of flow and joy, so as to be able to see the full picture and not only parts of it, and aspire to inner and not only outer perfection.

_____

(Change, erase, or pencil in those traits that you would like to change in yourself.)

This energy flows like a waterfall over your head. At the top of your head (crown chakra) an imaginary orifice is opened, through which the energy will flow through your body. Think of all the things you'd like to achieve and gaze at the mandala and take five breaths.

Close your eyes for a moment and imagine your life changing accordingly. In your mind, let today's special energy flow to everyone who is important to you. Count another five deep breaths and open your eyes.

Libra—September 23 to October 23

First, reread the introduction to this section: Your Birthday: The Most Special Day of the Year.

People born under the sign Libra find it hard to make decisions. Even when you have decided, you are not satisfied with your decision and argue with yourself over whether you did the right thing or not. You were born in a month full of positive energy that helps you in life and makes you a special person. If you learn to love every decision you make, you'll be much happier. The relaxation methods in the section "How Can I Stop My Thoughts While Meditating?" in the first chapter, Getting Started, contain ways for calming your feverish thoughts and alleviating the frequent headaches from which you suffer.

In order to feel as if you have both your feet on the ground, gaze at length at the mandala and draw its colors into your body, even if you don't practice the contents of the meditation, and not only on your birthday.

Meditation

Gaze at the center of the mandala and take ten deep breaths into your abdomen.

Imagine the skies opening and a special energy flowing down over you, so that you can make decisions more easily; so that you'll know that an occasional mistake is all right; so that you can accept every decision you make; and be connected to your inner peace and feel more secure and relaxed with those who are close to you.

(Change, erase, or pencil in those traits that you would like to change in yourself.)

This energy flows like a waterfall over your head. At the top of your head (crown chakra) an imaginary orifice is opened, through which the energy will flow through your body. Think of all the things you'd like to achieve and gaze at the mandala and take five breaths.

Close your eyes for a moment and imagine your life changing accordingly.

In your mind, let today's special energy flow to everyone who is important to you.

Count another five deep breaths with the color blue and open your eyes.

Scorpio—October 24 to November 21

First, reread the introduction to this section: Your Birthday: The Most Special Day of the Year.

People born under the sign of Scorpio have great mystical abilities; they are able to look into the future and to easily identify the weak points of the person before them; all this, in order to navigate things to their own benefit. Unlike people born under Sagittarius, half of whom are naive and don't really mean to shoot from the hip, Scorpio's arrows are aimed and put on hold until the right moment arises, when they are shot with predetermined accuracy. You don't usually feel sorry about your hurtful arrows. It's a trait that spoils everything you are about to get from the universe, what is due to you, because the energy you are trying to get through devious ways inevitably boomerangs right back to you. It is also the reason for your life being full of ups and, especially downs—pure survival. Your upcoming birthday presents a perfect opportunity to try to be less of a Scorpion and to find alternative, more positive, ways in order to receive (rather than to achieve, to grab, or to survive) what the universe wants to grant you.

Meditation

Gaze at the mandala and take ten deep breaths into your abdomen.

Imagine the skies opening and a special energy flowing down to you, to enable you to give from your heart, with no hidden agenda and to accept in the same way.

Ask for the energy to turn you into someone who is more positive and to be happier and content with what you have, to feel loved and secure all day long, and to let go of the control you have over everything and everyone.

(Change, erase, or pencil in those traits that you would like to change in yourself.)

This energy flows like a waterfall over your head. At the top of your head (crown chakra) an imaginary orifice is opened, through which the energy will flow through your body. Think of all the things you'd like to achieve and gaze at the mandala as you take five breaths.

Close your eyes for a moment and imagine your life changing accordingly.

In your mind, let today's special energy flow to everyone who is important to you.

Count another five deep breaths with the color blue and open your eyes.

The Art of Mandala Meditation

Sagittarius—November 22 to December 21

Don't jump to the middle of the page! First, reread the introduction to this section: Your Birthday: The Most Special Day of the Year.

People born under the sign of Sagittarius are prone to extraordinary slips of the tongue. After such a slip, you try hard to gather back all the words you said inadvertently, but it's usually too late. Sagittarians are forever in need of new challenges. Challenge is the only thing that motivates you and, as soon as you have achieved your objective, you lose interest in the process—although, as we all know, it's perseverance that brings results. The jobs you choose should not be connected to an office, so that you can also find your freedom at work. I suggest you explain to those closest to you that you need to be alone sometimes, so that your relationships will be much better.

Meditation

Gaze at the mandala and breathe deeply into your abdomen ten times.

Imagine the skies opening and releasing a flow of special energy down on you, to enable you to think of the word "patience" and make it a part of you; to enable you to stop for a moment before making a decision; to enable you to wait a minute before speaking an unsuitable expletive; and, instead of barraging those you love with the truth, the whole truth, and nothing but the truth, to enable you to provide them with the message in a way that suits them.

This energy will help you take advantage of your natural talent for conquering your objectives easily and help you locate positive targets for the arrows you release.

(Change, erase, or pencil in those traits that you would like to change in yourself.)

This energy flows like a waterfall over your head. At the top of your head (crown chakra) an imaginary orifice is opened, through which the energy will flow through your body. Think of all the things you'd like to achieve, gaze at the colors of the mandala, and take five breaths. Close your eyes for a moment and imagine your life changing accordingly. In your mind, let today's special energy flow to everyone who is important to you. Count another five deep breaths with the color blue and open your eyes.

Capricorn—December 22 to January 20

First, reread the introduction to this section: Your Birthday: The Most Special Day of the Year.

Although you may find this difficult to understand, it is on your birthday that your full potential emerges and you are given a chance to connect to what you really want, the desire that motivates you to work hard, in the hope that one day you will succeed big-time. The secret is that you don't need to work so hard in order to succeed; you can be helped by the power of thought and meditation, since it's there where it all begins—in your mind. People born under the sign of Capricorn are analytical, and for you everything has to be based on facts. In order to be able to see and identify the miracles that happen each day in your lives and to connect to them and, in order to understand that there really is a superpower at work on everyone's behalf, I suggest you listen to tales of miracles that have happened to others and accept them as fact. By connecting to miracles and the supernatural, you will come closer to real wealth and prosperity in all spheres of your life.

Meditation

Gaze at the center of the mandala and take ten deep breaths into your abdomen.

Imagine the skies opening and releasing a flow of energy down on you, an energy that will enable you to practice this meditation without doubts; that will provide you with peace of mind, even if you don't have a few million dollars in the bank; that will enable you to understand that you, too, deserve a break sometimes; and that will enable you to connect with your spiritual side and listen to your soul.

(Change, erase, or pencil in those traits that you would like to change in yourself.)

This energy flows like a waterfall over your head. At the top of your head (crown chakra) an imaginary orifice is opened, through which the energy will flow through your body. Think of all the things you'd like to achieve and gaze at the colors of the mandala and take five breaths. Close your eyes for a moment and imagine your life changing accordingly.

In your mind, let today's special energy flow to everyone who is important to you.

Count another five deep breaths while breathing the colors and open your eyes.

The Art of Mandala Meditation

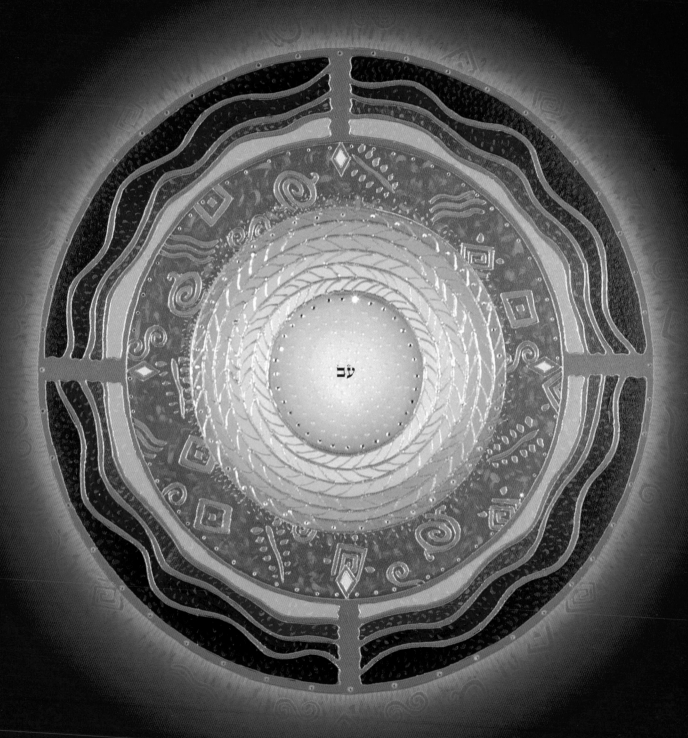

Aquarius—January 21 to February 18

First, reread the introduction to this section: Your Birthday: The Most Special Day of the Year.

People born under the sign of Aquarius wake up every morning with a brilliant idea in their heads. Good for you! Except you are incapable of implementing and putting into action any of these ideas, and this makes you quite frustrated. You must understand that the energy with which you came into the world has the ability to attract ideas. In this puzzle of life, implementation of your ideas is imposed upon other people, such as those born under the signs of Capricorn and Taurus—real workers, to whom you should connect and with whom you should cooperate. Only in this way can you implement your potential and be reconciled with yourself.

You should become closer to your family (wife/husband and children), spend as much time as possible at home with your children, and talk less and listen to them more as you allow them to express themselves.

Meditation

Gaze at the mandala, while counting ten deep breaths into your abdomen.

Imagine the skies opening and releasing a flow of special energy all over you, an energy that will allow you to implement the wonderful ideas you wake up with every morning; an energy that will allow you to internalize, to understand, and to see the people who are closest to you; an energy that will place you firmly on the ground and help you to be organized, in order to succeed in life.

(Change, erase, or pencil in those traits that you would like to change in yourself.)

This energy flows like a waterfall over your head. At the top of your head (crown chakra) an imaginary orifice is opened, through which the energy will flow through your body.

Think of all the things you'd like to achieve, gaze at the colors, and take five breaths.

Close your eyes for a moment and imagine your life changing accordingly.

In your mind, let today's special energy flow to everyone who is important to you.

Count another five deep breaths with the color red and open your eyes.

Pisces—February 19 to March 20

First, reread the introduction to this section: Your Birthday: The Most Special Day of the Year.

People born under the sign of Pisces have a sense of humor and a captivating smile, and there is a reason for this: You have a kind of monopoly over and responsibility for the world's state of joy, happiness, and energy and an ability to influence them. The saying "With spring comes joy" applies so aptly to you. As a Pisces, you can, if you so decide, change the mood of every place you enter; it would be a good thing, therefore, for you to decide to be forever happy and to think positive thoughts.

You belong to the only Zodiac sign to whom sharing comes straight from the heart and the word "no" is not part of your vocabulary. This is because you were born this way and therefore have nothing to boast about. You have to learn to say "no" when something is not right for you. Everyone knows that you can be squeezed and you will give with love, so you are the only Zodiac sign who actually has the right to refuse sometimes.

Meditation

Gaze at the mandala and take ten deep breaths into your abdomen. Imagine the skies opening and a special energy flowing over you; energy that will enable you to be constantly connected to the energy of joy and happiness; energy that will allow you to distinguish between emotion and logic; energy of independence and absolute certainty; and energy that will allow you to say "no" when necessary.

(Change, erase, or pencil in those traits that you would like to change in yourself.)

This energy is flowing down like a waterfall over your head. At the top of your head (crown chakra) an imaginary orifice is opened, through which the energy will flow through your body.

Think of all the things you'd like to achieve as you gaze at the colors and take five breaths.

Close your eyes for a moment and imagine your life changing accordingly.

In your mind, let today's special energy flow to everyone who is important to you.

Count another five deep breaths with the color red and open your eyes.

The Tree: Connecting to Your Inner World

You can learn more about your personality by the appearance of the tree you connect to in this meditation. I suggest you read the meditation from beginning to end before practicing it, and to write down your experiences in a diary.

Note: It is quite normal if, at the end of the meditation, your legs are quite stiff, since they act like a tree trunk during the meditation. Shake them a little in order to release this feeling.

Meditation

Lie down as you meditate and place the book by your side. Refer back to it whenever you have forgotten the instructions.

Begin with the breathing exercise at the beginning of the part "Meditations for the Soul."

Breathe deeply and let the air flow into your feet as you take three deep breaths.

From your feet, send imaginary roots into the ground.

With your eyes closed, look at your roots: Are they long or short, broad or narrow, twisting or straight?

Connect to the tree's energy. Imagine your legs turning into a tree trunk. What kind of a tree trunk is it? Is it peeling, crooked, tall and strong, young like a sapling, or something else?

Now, spring branches and leaves from your hips, from your chest, from your hands, and from your head. What kind of a tree have you become? Feel the wind in your leaves and check the height of your tree.

Do you have fruit? Is anyone taking shelter in your shadow?

Check where you are growing: in a fruit grove? Alone on a hill? Near a water source? In the jungle? In the woods?

Connect to the energy of sharing, like that of the tree, and imagine this sharing is in your heart.

Slowly, fold the branches and leaves inward from your chest, your hands, your head, and your abdomen.

Relax the tree trunk, breathe into your legs and begin to feel them. Gather the roots into your feet and move your legs a little.

Breathe into your hands and move your fingers.

Reaccustom yourself to the room and open your eyes whenever you are ready.

You will find interpretations for each stage after the Forest meditation.

If you were not able to interpret your experience by yourself, describe your tree in minute detail, according to the stages in the meditation, and send it to *argaman@netvision.net.il*.

The Forest

This meditation will help you understand the stage of your life that you are currently living. This understanding will grant you the knowledge to make suitable changes for improving your life. You can practice this meditation every six months, in complete honesty with yourself, and I hope that you'll be able to see the changes that took place since the last time. Moreover, I hope you notice many changes, because if you don't, this would mean that you are not changing.

Sit on a comfortable, high-backed chair, in front of a writing table, and place a sheet of paper and a pen on the table.

Read step one of the meditation. Close your eyes and ponder what you have read, then write a detailed account of what you can see and continue to the next step.

Meditation

1. Imagine a forest and your place in relation to it: Are you inside it, outside it, above it? What is the weather; warm and humid, wintery, rainy, snowy, a nice spring day? Are the trees crowded together or sparse? Is it a jungle, a large forest, a grove, or something else? What do you feel in this forest—fear, fun, calm, tension?
2. Does it have one path, or several footpaths, or do you have to forge your way forward through undergrowth?
3. As you walk, you come upon an obstacle: a brick wall, an abyss, a dangerous bridge, a small puddle, a hill, etc. Which obstacle was it? How did you choose to overcome it?
4. After getting around the obstacle, you encounter a bear. What does the bear look like? Does it attack you or does it like you? Are you afraid of it? Find

a way of bypassing the bear and moving forward. What action did you take?

5. You continue walking; on the ground you see a key. What does it look like? Is it ancient, small, large, rusty? Do you choose to take it with you or to leave it behind?

6. Continue walking. A dog appears before you. Is it glad to see you? What kind of dog is it? What does it look like? Is it patient, relaxed, barking, nervous, aggressive? Does it join you? If so, does it precede you, follow you, or walk alongside you?

7. Further along the path you see a jug. Where is the jug—on the side of the path, in its center? What condition is it in? Is it sunk in the ground, cracked, or whole? What shape is it? Is it painted or embellished? What colors and what embellishments does it have? Now walk closer to the jug and have a look inside it—what does it contain? If you don't want to look inside, point this out in your reply.

8. Keep walking until you reach a water source—a waterfall, a river, a hot or cold spring, a dry riverbed, or something else. What have you come to? How do you feel in this place? Are you there alone?

What are you doing? Are you drinking, going into the water, swimming, or passing by it to get to the next objective on the route?

9. You continue walking and see a cave. What do you feel—fear, curiosity, indifference? Do you choose to enter the cave? It's okay if you don't enter, write this on your answers page and end the meditation. If you did enter, note what you see and end the meditation.

You'll find interpretations to all the stages after the interpretations of the Tree meditation.

If you were unable to interpret your meditation on your own, I'd be happy to help. Describe the various stages of your forest route in great detail, in the order dictated by the meditation, and send to *argaman@netvision.net.il*.

Interpretation of the Tree Meditation

The tree represents a person. The person, too, has roots, from which he draws his traits and his personality. The deeper and more complex the roots, the more intense the person's involvement with the past. There also exists a connection between having both your feet on the ground and the thickness of the roots, and thus between the kind of connection and your home life.

Twisted roots symbolize a life full of challenge. Thin roots—these are usually found in young children, or people who are not deeply connected to their close family circle, or who spend most of their time on the move.

The tree trunk develops in this meditation along the length of your legs. The more upright and broad it is, the more it testifies to greater spiritual and mental strength, to the ability to cope with hardship, and to overall stability.

The bark symbolizes your spiritual age, the things you have been through in your life, and your attitude to your age.

The branches grow out of and spread throughout your upper body and teach you about your ability to create things and to your ability to share (shade, leaves, fruit, a shelter for birds, and for children at play).

Fruit-bearing trees testify to a sense of continuity, to emotional contentment, and the ability to see the fruits of your efforts in life.

Birds and children symbolize the ability to care for others and good connections with people around you. A swing—if it is not too heavy, or dislocates your arm—also shows a caring for others.

Butterflies symbolize vivid imagination and creativity.

Of no less importance is the location of the tree in its surroundings: A tree that is a long way away from

any others, or is alone on a hill, symbolizes loneliness or the choice to be alone. A jungle location symbolizes involvement in the way you live your life.

Streams of water are symbols of a person who shares with and is concerned about others, a person who lives a prosperous life.

Types of Trees

Fruit trees are symbolic of people who are friendly, who usually don't break down boundaries, who are not rebellious, who are organized, and who are content with their lives.

Cypress trees symbolize people who are lonely or prefer their own company, who are upright in themselves and introverts. They stick to their objectives and are resistant to the storms of life.

Oak trees symbolize a person who can be relied upon; one who really does feel upright, strong, and taller than everyone else.

A vine is symbolic of people who are special and humble.

Palm trees symbolize freedom lovers, people who are hard to approach, or those with a façade of being unapproachable. These people are special and creative and try to protect their sensitive personality.

A wide tree with widespread branches, open and full of leaves, hints at an open and sociable personality, full of joie de vivre, vitality, and constant renewal.

If the description of your tree is completely different from all the aforementioned, you are welcome to write to me; I will be happy to help: *argaman@netvision.net.il*.

Interpretation of the Forest Meditation

1. The forest is a symbol of your life as it is today. For example, if your general feeling in the forest is good and happy, with the sun shining and a pastoral atmosphere, this means that you are flowing and satisfied with your life. A feeling of suffocation in the forest, a fear of entering it, dark clouds, and rain, all describe a sense of suffocation in your life. It is positive to see small animals in the forest (or even tigers, if they are fond of you).

2. The path symbolizes the way in which you are coping with the process of your life. A single path testifies to a secure road, but also shows you might be stuck in your ways. It is better when there are additional, alternative paths. Too many paths (above four) sometimes signify an inability to decide and an excess of options.

3. The obstacle symbolizes the bureaucracy in your life. It is best to pass the obstacle with ease. It is also a positive sign if you pass it with help, so long as you pass it.

4. The bear symbolizes the enemies in your life and the way in which you cope with them. Just as you deal with the bear in your meditation, so do you deal with similar situations in your life.

5. The key symbolizes your past. If it is heavy, large, and rusty and you still choose to take it with you on your journey, this means that you still need to work on shedding your past. A small key of any kind does not disturb the current pleasantness of your life.

6. The dog symbolizes your relationships and love life. The relationship between the dogs and their size symbolizes the relationship between two marital partners and the influence they have on each other. If one walks in front of the other—it is the first one who leads in your relationship. For obvious reasons, it is not a positive sign to see the dog in front of you as something threatening or frightening.

7. The jug is a symbol of your external and internal aspects. Now that you understand this, try renovating the jug, by painting it, restoring any missing pieces (if you found that), and placing it in the middle of the road. From an internal point of view, it is good to see things inside the jug that can be shared, such as water, honey, gold coins, oil, etc. If you find things like dry leaves, snakes, snakes' eggs, dirt, or emptiness, I suggest you take a course in self-awareness, healing, Kabbalah, or any other subject you can connect with, which will raise the level of your self-satisfaction.

8. The water source is symbolic of your attitude to sex. If you see yourself jumping straight into the water, swimming, and jumping about, this is how you behave in bed. If you dipped your finger in and found the water too cold and sat, watching, on the beach, this, too, is your attitude to sex. If you saw a stream or a brook, this too reflects your reality. (The inmates of the prison where I did volunteer work saw a dry riverbed.) I recommend heating up the water, turning it into a lovely Jacuzzi, and climbing in with love.

9. The cave is symbolic of your attitude to death. If you are afraid to enter—it is obvious—only you should know that there is nothing to be afraid of. If you went in and found extinguished bonfires, these symbolize people you loved who have died. If there is light in the cave, or a torch, this is a positive sign that you have a high level of self-awareness.

If your description of your forest is completely different from the above, you are welcome to write to me; I would be happy to help: *argaman@netvision.net.il.*

Creating Your Own Mandalas

Welcome to the world of mandalas! When you color mandalas, you begin to open up a creative channel that directly connects to your soul. A mandala has the potential to transform your awareness and radically change your life toward a spiritual dimension.

Provided with this book, you will find several mandala patterns that will help you begin your practice. Choose one that you are drawn to and simply color it in with colored pencils, markers, or crayons. As you color in the center of your mandala, it will simultaneously open your own center within your heart. This brings expanded feelings and your capacity to be creative is enhanced quickly and often dramatically.

Traditionally, "light" comes from the center of each mandala. So try using lighter colors near the center of the mandala to enhance the feelings and appearance of your mandala. Mandala painting looks better if you are careful with the colors and try to be neat.

Energies of Geometric Patterns

There is a reason that many mandalas show a circle in the midst of a square. The circle represents femininity, while the square represents masculinity. This design creates integration between your inner feminine (your heart) and your inner masculine (your mind). When the colors are "right," you'll feel a presence awaken in the mandala.

As you advance to the next stages of mandala painting/coloring, your "inner artist" begins to come alive within you. When you're designing or painting a mandala, you're creating your own world within yourself. At this time, your mind begins to transform into the "Divine" mind and your heart into the "Divine" heart, as they open more and more. The practice of painting and drawing mandalas is a spiritual path, and as an artist, you will experience higher consciousness as you paint. The mandala is now going to be your teacher and your vehicle to allow you to explore deeper realms within.

Mandalas and Healing

The Tibetans revere the mandala, as they understand the sacredness and the value of this spiritual art form. The Tibetans say that there is a healing energy vibration that extends about 8 feet in front of a mandala. You can actually feel the energy if you close your eyes and extend your hand toward the center of the mandala. The Dalai Lama says that in drawing mandalas, you are cultivating deeper consciousness and feelings in order to connect with yourself and the world in a more compassionate manner; therefore, all artists have a responsibility to transform and heal themselves and the world.

Let's start! Here are guidelines to painting each of the blank mandalas you'll find in the special insert within this book. You can easily tear out each template so you can color it more comfortably.

One-Day Mandala

This is a pattern for beginners. First, apply a light color to the entire page. Then begin laying on colors, from light in the center to darker near the edges. What works best in the beginning is to use just a few colors, for example, blues and purples or greens and yellows. The mandala will tell you immediately if the colors aren't right. Once you've layered the painting with colors, go back and adjust the colors until each one is in harmony. Don't forget to breathe!

Love Mandala

When you approach a love mandala, you're opening yourself to love. I suggest you start with a bright color and paint your way around this mandala. It helps to look at one or two love mandalas in the book and copy the colors. Remember: The more colors you use, the more you must learn to balance the relationships of your overall color scheme. This will come naturally if you continue to practice.

Nature Mandala

This mandala template is a wonderful example of painting as a way to open a deeper relationship with nature. I suggest you start with the green leaves or trees around the outside and then work your way toward the middle. Stay with greens and make this a personal tribute to your own nature. You can mix all greens in any shade together. Green is the color of the heart chakra or heart center, and green strengthens the heart and the immune system. But if green doesn't

feel right, by all means, go for blue or whatever color the mandala is asking for.

Flower of Life Mandala

This mandala contains only circles, which symbolize the feminine. So just "flow" into this mandala and try very soft colors, which represent the sensitivity of the feminine. It helps to use only two colors in this template, as the pattern looks better that way. I suggest using a darker color for the spaces between the petals and color the petals lighter. For example, color a dark blue background and light blue petals. As you're painting this mandala, you may notice that your feelings are expanding, "flowering." If you feel rushed for time, choose another mandala.

Heart Mandala

As you're coloring heart after heart, you open yourself to being more in touch with your own heart. This mandala lends itself to multicolor, so try coloring the background a soft, neutral color and then make the hearts as many bright colors as you like. Once you've finished, go up to everyone you love and appreciate in your life and give them a big, long hug. And don't forget to hug yourself!

Endless Knot Mandala

This is a difficult pattern, as the design doesn't end, it just continues endlessly. Make sure you color or paint this one slowly and carefully. It's a good pattern to try out the colors of the rainbow on—in other words, start with red in the center, then orange, then yellow, green, light blue, blue, and purple. These rainbow colors are also colors of your chakras, or energy centers that reveal levels of your energy body (see the first chapter, Getting Started). Paint this mandala three or four times in a row to practice the art of color relationships.

Sri Yantra Mandala

This pattern is considered the "Mother" of all mandalas and dates back at least 6,000 years. Yantra means that it's made essentially for meditation. By looking at any mandala or Yantra, you are meditating with your eyes open, or slightly open, as the Buddha is "always" depicted. The traditional way to paint this Yantra is to color all the triangles red (which represents the feminine color) and surround them with the color white, which represents the masculine. It's important with the Sri Yantra mandala to look at paintings or images of the symbol so you don't get lost inside this mandala!

Double Spiral Mandala

This mandala pattern represents the double spirals that can be seen in nature. For example, it is contained in the center of a sunflower as well as some seashells. This particular mandala has eight points and represents the path toward slowly opening your heart. This mandala always looks better if you blend colors and put the lightest and brightest ones at the center. For example, start out with very light blue at the center

and then gradually darken the blue as you move out from the center.

Final Thoughts

If you'd like to try to make your own mandala without one of the templates in this book, begin by using a compass to make circles. Make several circles within each other, always using the same middle point. Once you've done this, draw lotus petals or other geometric patterns around or within the circles. Make sure to divide your circles in equal parts so that your pattern comes out symmetrically.

For other ideas on mandala designs, visit our website, *www.mandalas.com*.

Have a fine, creative day!

Paul Heussenstamm

Recommended Reading

72 Names of God: Technology for the Soul, by Yehuda Berg, The Kabbalah Center

Becoming Like God, by Michael Berg, The Kabbalah Center

Love Is in the Earth, by Melody, Earth Love Publishing House

Messages from Water, by Dr. Masaru Emoto

A New Earth, by Eckhart Tolle

Perfect Health, by Deepak Chopra, The Complete Mind/Body Guide

The Power to Change Everything, by Yehuda Berg, The Kabbalah Center

The Secret, by Rhonda Byrne

Solomon's Angels, by Doreen Virtue

Spiritual Liberation: Fulfilling Your Soul's Potential, by Michael Bernard Beckwith

Vital Energy, by Dr. David Simon

You Can Heal Your Life, by Louise L. Hay

More about the Book *Divine Forces* by Paul Heussenstamm

DIVINE FORCES
Art that Awakens the Soul

Paul Heussenstamm
"OURtist"

"Archetypal manifestations of higher consciousness." - Deepak Chopra
"Mandalas that carry a presence that can heal." - Eckhart Tolle
"Metaphysical principles from which the Universe has emerged." - Rev. Michael Beckwith

By W. Brugh Joy, Life Teacher and Author of *Joy's Way* and *Avalanche: Heretical Reflections on the Dark and the Light*

To a teacher of life's mysteries, nothing excites the imagination more than when someone comes along who can illuminate the spiritual forces that underlie an activity. In this book, Paul Heussenstamm reveals art as a path into the spiritual realms where the artist is discovered and where the experiences of the heart chakra are known, integrated, and become modulating influences in the expression of the artist.

The uninitiated artist is an individual who has learned and developed certain skills to express a rendering of either the inner or outer world available to him or to her. The initiated artist knows that the inspiration and the signature expression come through as impulses or as a compulsion from something beyond the personal self. It is as if the person is the living vehicle of expression for a larger and more collective being. The more the individual surrenders to this call (transpersonal impulse), the greater is the power and endowment of the creation. The exposure to any work manifesting through this kind of artist can be enough to induct such a potential in the viewer. An even more powerful way is simply to hang out with the artist, whether through classes or as he or she artistically expresses this fascinating grace.

It is not a matter of asking questions or of learning technique. It has everything to do with riding along in the radiance of the artist operating through the person. An individual is indwelled and initiated by the forces moving through the artist.

For every great human expression, there are transpersonal equivalents that when accessed, transform the expression from the mundane to the sublime. We could then speak of the Healer, the Warrior, the Mother, the Father, the Teacher, the Child, and so on. In this book, Paul is addressing an approach to experience the grace of the Artist. It is a development that transforms the individual from a purely self-centered and egotistical expression and understanding of life to an individual who sacrifices the personal for the transpersonal awareness. In doing so, the individual is graced with resources, senses, and insights that can only be called awakened. As Paul reveals, the artist cannot be willed, nor can it be forced into development. This is the mystery.

One can only be graced by its presence and then only through a sacrifice of self-centeredness. The action into the artist involves surrender, letting go, allowing, opening, petitioning, prayer, and inner supplication. Although this is the usual path to prepare for the transformation, there are plenty of examples where the transformation took place spontaneously, without conscious participation of the individual. He or she simply wakes up to the fact that something larger than his or her own sense of self is operating inside and expressing itself through action in the world.

It is important to understand the difference between the artist who is occupied with artistic expression and the artist who is called, in the spiritual sense, to express a collective and transcendent mystery. The former is an unconscious reflection of the sacred that lies behind the artistic expression. The works are technically and skillfully expressed and meet, to a large measure, what we usually call art. The artist who is called enters the vocation (this word means to be called by divine inspiration) of the artist. It is not a choice, nor is it a willed expression. The individual is truly an instrument and realizes such.

What does the spiritual path of the artist have to do with such an esoteric realization as the experience of the transpersonal through the heart center or chakra?

First, the definition of the state of consciousness as experienced through the transpersonal forces of the heart center needs to be considered.

Thousands of years ago, the Eastern approach to spirituality differentiated the several states of awareness available to the individual in his or her path of spiritual realization. Each of the levels or aspects of consciousness are distinct and quite beyond the surface of ordinary human awareness. To achieve realization of any of these states of consciousness is a lifelong discipline, requiring enormous sacrifice of one's ordinary human expression. The states of awareness are associated with radiant forces emanating from different levels of the physical body. Each of the states of awareness associated with the energy centers of the body is transpersonal, beyond the ordinary consciousness, and operates independently of the surface consciousness.

The heart chakra or center forces are, for Paul and many others, a profoundly moving and appropriate preparation to becoming an instrument or a living incarnation of the artist. The ego undergoes a change from a me-and-mine-centered awareness to an us-and-ours dimensionality of being. The ego suffers a deflation, yet in doing so becomes a much larger carrier of the deeper mysteries of life. The heart center experience is therefore a development where the surface consciousness becomes aware of the larger, more transcendental aspects of life and places its resources in service to this larger mystery. The heart center is not a personal state of consciousness; it is impersonal, yet deeply feeling.

Of the two transcendent or spiritual states of awareness available to most Westerners, the mind and the heart, the heart expresses in the reality of relationships rather than in differentiation and discernment realities. The artist knows innately the relationship of color, form, composition, feeling, and meaning without the need for words or concepts. It is through the whole that the experience comes and not through its parts. In Paul's case, the artist's eye becomes available. The larger dimensional relationships of life and objects are seen in new ways completely unavailable to the surface eye.

All anyone has to do to experience the power of creative genius is to enter Paul Heussenstamm's home. On wall after wall are the products of his vocation—his call into being a vehicle through which the artist expresses.

These are not works of art that Paul possesses. Rather, they possess him. It is in this sense that the capital "A" of the Artist as discussed in this section and in this book is to be understood. To capitalize the word "Artist" is to reveal its spiritual basis. Again, the artist refers to the demon or genie, a transcendental, overarching influence, to which any great artist surrenders and that guides the unfolding and development of the expression. It does not refer to the person who submits to such forces. The person as a vehicle is the artist but is not the artist. It is the spiritual aspect, the transcendent aspect, of being an artist that Paul so richly explores in his book. In our culture, we speak of those individuals who are inspired beyond the ordinary as masters. Paul is an unfolding master.

I am a very appreciative witness of Paul's path of artistic spiritual expression. His creative flow expressed in his paintings has augmented most of my conferences over the past twenty-five years, constantly inducting and communicating the deeper soul mysteries to the attending participants. His famous mandalas, uniquely conceived soul portraits of individuals, grace many homes throughout the country. The essential nature of a mandala is to express the core or heart of the matter in question. Paul lets go of his head and moves to his heart center for the images that will become that person's mandala. He is given the artist's eye to know the individual on a transcendent level.

The divinity of the mind would reach the core of anything it puts its mind to and will see the essential nature yet be unable to flesh out or humanize the realization. It would express in descriptions and concepts what the artist can and does express in images (relationship of forces that appear as images). Ah, the truth of "a picture is worth a thousand words."

And what I most appreciate about Paul, more than the paintings themselves, is his beingness, an extremely fertile, dynamic, and living artistic rendering, an actual incarnation of the artist who inspires and inducts through color, passion, word and body, lovemaking, touch, dress, and physical presence. The artist makes love to the world through Paul. And we, including Paul, are its lovers.

W. Brugh Joy

One-Day Mandala

Love Mandala

Nature Mandala

Flower of Life Mandala

Heart Mandala

Endless Knot Mandala

Sri Yanta Mandala

Double Spiral Mandala